Mark in 40 Days

MARK IN 40 DAYS

Simon and Chris Danes

ST MARK'S PRESS

www.stmarkspress.com

CONTENTS

Preface

Mark in 40 Days offers a short Bible study course, either for individual use or for groups. As the text of the Gospel is divided into 40 sections, it's ideal for Lent but it can be used at any time during the year.

We've also included some introductory material to explain the background against which Mark was writing, and a few additional articles which explore some themes and ideas in more detail. They're designed as extra material and you may wish to skip over them if you simply want the Bible study material.

Simon and Chris Danes

Introduction

Before we start our study of Mark, it's worth considering the historical background to Jesus' time, what sort of a book Mark is (who wrote it, when and why), and the rather different approaches Christians today have to the Gospel.

Let's begin by looking at:

Life in the time of Jesus

The first thing to say is that the date of Jesus' birth was rather earlier than is usually thought!

The Anno Domini system was worked out in the sixth century by a monk called Dionysius Exiguus – and he got his sums wrong. We can't be absolutely certain, but it looks as though 4 BC is the most likely date for Jesus' birth. If it wasn't then, it was certainly close to that time. Jesus was crucified either in 29, 30 or 33 AD; again, it's impossible to sure which. That would make him between 33 and 37 when he died; perhaps a little older than is often thought.

By the time of Jesus' birth, Israel was part of the Roman Empire. In 37 BC, the Romans appointed Herod the Great to run Israel for them (this is the Herod who Matthew says ordered the killing of the children in Bethlehem when Jesus was born). Herod was ruthless and paranoid, and the Jews hated him. When he died in 4 BC, the Romans divided his kingdom between three of his sons. Two of them are relevant to the study of Mark:

Herod Archelaus, who ruled the southern part of Israel: Judea. Even by the standards of the Herod family, he was a thug and an incompetent, so the Romans sacked him and replaced him with a Roman governor: the procurator or prefect. The best known is Pontius Pilate. In fact, while the Gospels call him the 'procurator', this seems to have been a later title for the post; Pilate in his own day would have been called 'prefect', and this is confirmed by an inscription found in Caesarea in 1966. Some of the inscription has been worn away, but it seems to have read 'Pontius Pilate, prefect of Judea'. (The Gospels call him 'procurator' because, when they were writing, this was the correct title for the governor. It started being used from AD 44.) Pilate was a hard line, no nonsense soldier.

Herod Antipas ruled **Galilee**, the northern part of Israel. The Romans wouldn't allow him the title 'king', so he was known as the 'tetrarch'. Like his brother and his dear old dad, Antipas was not the most shining example of humanity.

While the Romans outlawed some religions in the Empire, they allowed the Jews to continue to practise their faith. Three things that were important to the Jews in their everyday lives were the Torah, the synagogue and the Temple. These feature in Mark and need some explanation.

The **Torah** was and is the heart of the Jewish faith. The Jews believed that God had given his laws to Moses; in fact, the word *Torah* means 'law' or 'instruction'. The five books of the Torah, the first five books of the Christian Old Testament, were said to have been written by Moses himself, who recorded God's laws for the Jews for later generations.

The Torah is also sometimes called the Pentateuch, the Law (it's usually called this in English Bibles) or the Law of Moses.

The **synagogue** was the local place of worship, where the Torah was read and explained. There was a synagogue in every town and in most villages; they also acted as a school and a community centre.

Literacy levels were high in first Century Israel; Jesus, like every other male Jew, would have been able to read and write.

While there were many synagogues, there was only one **Temple**. The Old Testament says that King David, who was the second king of Israel, wanted to build a temple in his newly conquered city of Jerusalem, but the honour went to his son Solomon. (Solomon reigned 970-910 BC.) Solomon's Temple was eventually pulled down by the Babylonian army in 587, when the Jewish political state of Judah was destroyed and the Jews were taken off to exile in Babylon. (It was during this period that much of the Old Testament was written down.) Then the Babylonian Empire was itself destroyed by the Persians, and the king of Persia, Cyrus, allowed the Jews to return home. Once they returned, they rebuilt the Temple on the same site, and it was this Temple that Jesus knew. Herod the Great added to the buildings to make them even more impressive. As the Jews believed that God had told Solomon to build the Temple, it was the holiest place in the world. Much of the Torah deals with the rituals surrounding animal sacrifices and it was only at the Temple that these sacrifices were offered.

Jews today still have the Torah and synagogues, but they do not have the Temple. The Romans destroyed it in the Jewish War of 70 AD and it has never been rebuilt. The site remains holy for modern Jews. A huge mosque called the Dome of the Rock, a Muslim shrine, stands there today.

*

If we were asked today to explain what Christianity is, we'd probably find it fairly straightforward to explain the core beliefs about God, Jesus, the idea of Christian love and so on, but after that we'd soon run into difficulties. Not all Christians believe exactly the same things, and some of the more hard line Christians would say that anyone who disagrees with them isn't really a Christian at all. Some Christians believe the Bible is infallible, others that the Pope is infallible, and still others that we nothing can be infallible in a human world. So it's quite hard to say, 'All Christians believe that...' It's similar, too, when talking about Jewish beliefs in the time of Jesus. There may be a core set of beliefs, but there were different emphases within Judaism – and, as there are extremists within any religion nowadays, there were extremists then too.

Many Jews belonged to one of four groups: Pharisees, Sadducees, Zealots and Essenes. If you didn't strictly speaking 'belong' to one of these groups, you might still identify more with one than with another. It's a bit like to political parties today: people might call themselves 'conservatives' or 'liberals' or 'labour' but that need not mean they've actually paid their sub and are card carrying party members. If you like, there's a level of commitment. So, in first century Israel, you might call yourself a Pharisee because you prefer the Pharisees' line to any other but you're not actually a fully paid up member of the group, as it were.

So what did the different groups believe?

The **Pharisees** formed the largest group. It's not absolutely certain what their name means, but it probably means 'the separated ones', as though they kept themselves apart from those who didn't follow their rules.

Their main aim was to keep the laws of the Torah. Some of them studied it full-time, but others had normal jobs as well. They tried to make sure the laws of the Torah were always kept by 'making a fence around the Law', which meant they had extra rules to make sure they did not even break the Law by accident. These rules, and there were thousands of them, were learnt by heart.

For example, the ten commandments in the Torah say that no one should work on the Sabbath (Exodus 20.8). This law was presumably designed to give people a day off from work so they could rest and worship. But the Pharisees were desperate to make sure it was always kept. So they said people could not do *anything* on the Sabbath that might mean 'work'. They said you could not walk more than two-thirds of a mile, and could not even write on the Sabbath. Rules like these got more and more difficult to keep.

Most Pharisees were genuinely religious people who wanted to try to keep the Torah, to please God, and to serve their fellow human beings. Mark and the other Gospels are rather hard on them, perhaps unfairly. You don't have to read Mark for very long before you can sense his frustration with those Jews who wouldn't believe in Jesus, and this may lead him to exaggerations. And lots of them did accept Jesus: Paul, the great early Christian missionary, was a Pharisee. So was Nicodemus, one of Jesus' earliest followers in John's Gospel.

The Pharisees accepted some other doctrines (religious teachings) that were not in the Torah, but were in the other books that now make up the Jewish Bible or Old Testament. They believed in angels, life after death – and in the coming of the Messiah.

(We talk about the Jewish Bible or the Old Testament in connection with Jesus' time, but in fact it was a bit more fluid than that. The Jews' Bible was not yet fixed. Some wanted to limit it to just a few books; others included not just the books that we now have, but a great many writings which were later rejected. While all the Jews accepted that there was such a thing as scripture, they didn't all agree yet which books were scripture and which weren't.)

The **Sadducees** were a very small group. Most of them were priests in the Temple. They were generally very well off, they enjoyed being at the top of the tree in society, and they looked down on ordinary people. They did not want trouble with the Romans because this might affect their power.

The precise meaning of their name is uncertain, but it may mean the 'sons of Zadok'. (Zadok had been a priest under King David, a thousand years before.) 'Sons of Zadok' roughly translates as 'members of the priests' party'.

The Sadducees based their thinking entirely on the Torah and rejected doctrines that were not in it. So, they did not believe in angels, the Messiah, or life after death. (Mark says they had an argument with Jesus about the last of these; see Mark 12.18-27.) So their religion was rather different from that of the Pharisees, who they consequently disliked. They rejected the Pharisees' additions to the Law. For them, the Torah was sufficient.

(In Jesus' parable of the rich man and Lazarus in Luke's Gospel (16.19-31), Jesus probably means the rich man is a Sadducee. If you look at the parable carefully, you'll notice a number of clues to this: he wears expensive purple clothes and has a huge amount of money;

he doesn't seem to have been aware that life after death was a real possibility, and wants his brothers to be warned about it; and Abraham reminds him that his brothers should listen to 'Moses' (who, if they were Sadducees, they would) *'and* the prophets' (who they would ignore, as they rejected anything not in the Torah. Life after death does not feature in the Torah but it does in the prophets' writings.)

The **Zealots:** By AD 66, there was a Jewish religious group or sect called 'the Zealots'. The word is also used to describe those Jews in Jesus' time who were fanatically opposed to Roman rule, and who even called for armed resistance to Rome. In Jesus' day, though, there was not *one* Zealot movement, but several. We can use 'Zealot' as a convenient label for these resistance movements. Some of these people were also Pharisees. None was a Sadducee because the Roman occupation suited the Sadducees very nicely.

The Romans considered the Zealots to be terrorists; many Jews thought they were freedom fighters. They hated being ruled by foreigners who were not members of God's holy people. They were waiting for the Messiah who would lead them into battle.

One of Jesus' disciples was Simon 'the Zealot'. The name may just mean he was a zealous person, but it's generally thought he was a Zealot in the other sense of the word. Some scholars would say that Judas Iscariot was a Zealot too. The evidence isn't as strong as for Simon but it certainly fits: if he was expecting a political and military liberator, he would have become very disillusioned by Jesus and this would give him the motive for betraying him. Moreover, his surname may be a corruption of *sicarii* or 'dagger-bearer'.

Mark says Barabbas, who the crowd chose instead of Jesus, had committed murder 'during the uprising' (15.7). If this was a political act of violence, it would make Barabbas a Zealot. Again, it certainly fits.

The **Essenes** were rather like monks. While some lived in towns, most lived in the desert in Judea. The Dead Sea Scrolls, a collection of books discovered at Qumran in 1948, were either written by an Essense community or by a group who were very like the Essenes. They believed all the other Jews had gone away from what God wanted; they alone were the true Jews. Because of this, their rules were very strict: much stricter than those of the Pharisees. Many did not marry; when they did, it was only to produce children. The Dead Sea Scrolls say that it took two years of hard training to become a member of the Qumran community. After that, they gave up all their possessions and shared all they had with the other members of the group. They were expecting a supernatural war between 'the sons of light' (themselves!) and 'the sons of darkness', who included demons but also means 'people who the Essenes do not like'.

The Essenes aren't mentioned directly in any of the Gospels. This isn't surprising; if they kept themselves to themselves, they probably would have had little contact with other religious teachers, including Jesus himself. However, because there are similarities between their teachings and those of John the Baptist – the Essenes practised baptism, although for them it was a repeated ritual, and they believed a terrible judgement was at hand – it's sometimes been suggested that John himself may for a time have been an Essene. If he was, though, he would have left the group before the time he appears in Mark.

The Romans did allow the Jews a little power to run their own affairs. The **Sanhedrin**, the Jewish council, existed to control religious matters, and it had some authority to act as a criminal court. Jesus appeared before the Sanhedrin when he was on trial for his life. The Temple's High Priest (a man called Caiaphas in Jesus' time) was the chairman. Its other seventy members were Sadducees, Pharisees, and **scribes**.

The **scribes** are also called **teachers of the Law** or **doctors of the Law** in some English Bibles. Their main job was to teach the Torah. Many of them were Pharisees, though some were Sadducees. Jewish literature usually calls them **rabbis**. Scribes who were also Pharisees were particularly keen on making sure the Torah was never broken. They added a number of new laws, called the Oral Law (the spoken Torah, as opposed to the written Torah). We have seen how the Pharisees ensured that people did not break the commandment to keep the Sabbath holy. The scribes wanted to know whether the commandment just meant going out to work, or any work at all. Some rabbis said it *did* mean anything that you could call work: writing, setting broken bones, carrying a needle in your robe if you were a tailor. If someone asked a scribe a question about the Torah, he would usually reply, 'There is a teaching which says...' so and so. Rather like lawyers today, they backed up what they said by referring back to what someone else had said. Jesus' interpretation of the Torah was different from most of the scribes', and they did not like it.

(There is, though, an example of a scribe agreeing with Jesus in Mark 12.28-34. This is worth reading; it shows Jesus and the scribe discussing the Torah as two first Century rabbis would have done.)

Mark: who, what, why, where and when?

The word 'gospel' comes from Old English. It is a translation of the
Greek word *euangelion*, which means Good News. The earliest
Christians believed that the story of Jesus' life, death and resurrection
was *good news* for people who accepted it, because it promised them a
new sort of life on earth, and the hope of heaven after death. The
first meaning of 'gospel', then, is the message of good news about
Jesus.

For thirty years or so after Jesus' crucifixion, the gospel was mainly
something that was spoken rather than written. Most of Jesus' first
followers were still alive, and they spread the good news about him
by their teaching. At most, they had notebooks to remind their
helpers of the things Jesus had said, and the order of events which led
up to his death. As time went on, however, what we know as the
four Gospels of the New Testament came to be written.

There were three main reasons why this happened:

1. The earliest disciples of Jesus began to die off. There was a
   need to write down their teaching about Jesus before it was
   forgotten.
2. Christianity was growing very fast among people who had all
   sorts of religious backgrounds. The evangelists thought there
   was a danger that some of them might bring wrong ideas –
   heresies – with them into the Church. The Gospels were
   written to prevent this from happening.
3. Christians were being persecuted by the Roman and Jewish
   authorities. The Gospel writers wanted to show that there was
   no danger to Rome from Christianity and to encourage
   Christians to stand firm in their faith when they were under
   attack.

All four Gospels, like the rest of the New Testament, were written
in Greek, the language spoken throughout the Roman Empire. (It
was quite a lot later that the Christians started using Latin.) To save
paper, the text was written without punctuation or spaces between
the words. Older books about the Bible usually say that the Gospels
were written on scrolls but we now know this may not have been the
case. What we would usually think of as a book – sheets of paper,
bound together – were available and Mark may have used one. The
chapter and verse numbers aren't original. They were added over a
thousand years later (though it is uncertain exactly when), to make it
easier for people to find their way around the Bible. They can be

misleading because they sometimes mark breaks or sections in a text which may not reflect the writers' intentions.

While the Gospels contain a lot of stories about what Jesus said and did, they leave out things we would expect a modern biographer to tell us. They don't even tell us what Jesus looked like. Mark tells us nothing about Jesus' childhood or education, and hardly anything about his family.

All this is because the Gospels are the Christian *message* about Jesus. In a sense they were biographies; they do tell Jesus' life story, or at least part of it. But they tend to ignore things that aren't directly relevant to the message. As a result, they're silent on a lot of things that we might now like to know, but which for them were pretty unimportant.

Who wrote Mark?

Not an easy question to answer.

Christian tradition, going back many centuries, says he was the same Mark (or John Mark) who appears in stories and letters in other parts of the New Testament. If this is right, then we know that his home was in Jerusalem, that his mother's name was Mary, and that he set out with Paul on the apostle's first missionary journey (Acts 12.12, 13.1-5). There must have been some sort of quarrel, because Mark left the expedition early and went home. For a while, Paul would have nothing more to do with him (Acts 15.37-40), but eventually they patched it up, and Paul talked about him in his later letters (Colossians 4.10, Philemon 24).

There's a very strong early tradition which links Mark with Peter. Papias, writing just under 100 years after Jesus' crucifixion, claims an even early Christian leader told him:

> Mark was not one of Jesus' original followers, but he was Peter's assistant.

Papias said that Mark wrote down the stories Peter told about Jesus while Peter was preaching. In the New Testament, the First Letter of Peter talks about 'my son Mark'.

It sounds good, but should we take Papias' word for it? Some New Testament scholars think Papias has got it right; others suspect he's guessing.

To begin with, 'Mark' or 'Marcus' was one of the commonest names in the Roman Empire. It's not *certain* that the John Mark of

Acts is the same person as the Mark of Paul's letters, or the Mark in the First Letter of Peter. There must have been lots of other Marks in the early Church.

Moreover, many scholars think Peter didn't really write the First Letter of Peter. If so, it's not much help as evidence. However, the idea that Peter *did* write it is becoming more popular among many experts – but we haven't the space to explore the problem here.

And whoever wrote Mark frequently does not seem to know where places in Judea and Galilee are; he gets his geography wrong. This would be odd if he were John Mark, whose home was in Jerusalem. (Or would it? How many British people know exactly where Penzance, Ebbw Vale, Leicester, Belfast and Carlisle are without looking at a map?)

But then a lot of stories in Mark are almost told from Peter's viewpoint. At least one story could, at the end of the day, only have come from him; he was the only follower of Jesus present at the time (see 14.66-72).

And yet, if Mark really knew Peter, wouldn't we get a lot more detail? Many of the accounts seem shorn down to the bare essentials, without the sort of detail you'd get from someone who was actually there. This suggests that, as they were told, the accounts were reduced to the bare bones to make them easier to commit to memory. It is argued that it was these 'boiled down' versions that Mark had access to, rather than an eyewitness.

(It's worth looking at Mark 1.29-31 and 2.23-27 and considering whether they look more like 'boiled down' accounts or reports of an eyewitness. What do you think?)

It has to be said it's hard to reach a firm conclusion. The early Christian writers all insist that John Mark, who knew Peter and recorded Peter's memories, was the writer of Mark. The tradition is very strong and Papias is very early. If we say John Mark was not the author, then we have no idea who the author was. Perhaps some scholars are reluctant to let go of Papias' testimony because, if Mark knew Peter, then Mark's going to be very accurate – and they want him to be accurate.

On the other hand, if Papias is wrong, and we don't know who wrote Mark, it doesn't follow that the Gospel is therefore inaccurate. It would depend of the quality of Mark's sources – and Peter was certainly not the only accurate source of information about Jesus in the earliest Church. And it has to be said that the date of Mark means he was writing when there were still eyewitnesses around, who could correct any errors. This brings us to:

When and where was Mark written?

Again, it's not possible to be certain, but there's a good case for saying Mark wrote in 64 AD, in Rome.

The date and the place certainly fit. The Emperor Nero – not the most balanced of individuals – decided to burn down large parts of the city so that he could gain the credit for rebuilding it. Ever the politician, Nero was very keen to blame his actions on somebody else. A new group had recently arrived in Rome. People didn't know much about them and some citizens regarded them with suspicion. The Roman historian Tacitus takes up the story:

> Nero fastened the guilt [for the fire he started in Rome] on a class hated for their abominations, called Christians by the people. He inflicted the most exquisite tortures on them. Christ, from whom they get their name, was executed during the reign of Tiberius at the hands of one of our procurators, Pontius Pilate. The mischievous superstition, held back for the moment, broke out again: not only in Judea, the source of the evil, but even in Rome itself.
>
> Tacitus, *Annals* 15.44.2-8

We know from the early Christian writers that Peter died during Nero's massacre. And there's a strong emphasis in Mark on standing firm in the face of persecution; 13.9-13 is just one example.

In any case, we know that it could not have been very much later than this. Matthew and Luke both used Mark as a source, and most scholars think both were writing around AD 80.

Saying Mark was written about AD 64-65, some thirty years after the crucifixion, is a safe bet.

Some experts would put it a little later; others suggest it is even earlier, perhaps AD 45. However, almost all scholars are sure that Mark is the earliest of the four Gospels. (It used to be thought that Matthew wrote first, which is why his work comes at the beginning of the New Testament. But this is not an easy position to defend and few now hold it.)

A Roman setting fits some of the other details in Mark. Mark explains Jewish customs to his readers. Jewish readers, perhaps in Palestine, wouldn't need this, but Gentile readers in Rome would find it useful. And Mark sometimes uses Latin words written in Greek characters instead of the correct Greek words. When Luke and Matthew are working from Mark, they correct this; it was seen as sloppy style. For example, Mark uses the Latin word 'centurion';

Luke, who has a better written style, uses a Greek word meaning 'the leader of a hundred men'. (On the other hand, does this really fix Mark in Rome? Surely using the odd Latin word would have been common throughout the Roman Empire?)

Where did Mark get his information from?

We have seen that some of Mark's stories may have come from Peter. But what other sources did he use?

The early Christians thought that the most important part of the story about Jesus was the series of events which led up to his death: the *passion narrative* ('passion' comes from the Greek 'pathein', 'to suffer'). The passion narrative was almost certainly the first part of the Gospel to be written down and it looks as though Mark was working from a written passion narrative when he was writing his account.

He may also have had a written source for what is now Mark chapter 13.

Jesus' first language was Aramaic, a language related to Hebrew. By the first century, Palestinian Jews spoke Aramaic as their first language, though Hebrew was used in the synagogue. (As a result, Jesus would have known Hebrew, and would have found it difficult to get work as a carpenter if he didn't know at least some Greek. We now know that there was a trading centre called Sepphoris in Galilee, where business was conducted with Greek speaking Gentiles; it's likely that Jesus would have conducted some business there.) It's likely, too, that there were early collections of sayings of Jesus, written in Aramaic, their original language. Notebooks like these may well have been common. Mark's Greek is not very good. English translations usually iron this out, but he writes in a breathless, jerky kind of way, almost as a child would write. It makes it look as though Mark's first language was not Greek. Some scholars suggest Mark often writes as though he has translated something from Aramaic; just occasionally, he uses Aramaic words. So, perhaps behind Mark's Gospel there are written stories in Aramaic. That would make them very early indeed, and historically very valuable; the early Church very quickly switched to Greek once Christianity moved outside of Israel. And Aramaic was Peter's first language, too.

The sayings of Jesus would have been handed down by word of mouth and memorized. This was the normal way of learning in Mark's time, when books were very expensive. In the West, we tend today not to commit vast swathes of material to memory because we're so reliant on documents. We can therefore be overly suspicious of relying on oral transmission: because we're not usually very good at it, we can assume that the memory's not an accurate tool and that any word of mouth transmission is like Chinese whispers. This isn't true. There are many cultures where memorising texts is still greatly prized, and the fact that actors in the West can still commit entire plays of Shakespeare to memory shows that, when it's trained, the memory can be perfectly accurate.

How accurate is the Gospel?

This is part of the whole question of the authority of the Bible. There are Christians, of course, who believe that every word Mark wrote is totally accurate and that God the Holy Spirit prevented him from making a single error. This view, sometimes (and perhaps not very kindly) called fundamentalism, has a long pedigree; many of the early Christian writers assumed that the individual Biblical writers were little more than secretaries, writing down what God dictated.

Today, most Christians would not go as far as this. They would accept that human beings played their part in writing the Gospels, and human beings make mistakes. However, they wouldn't go so far as to say that these mistakes were major or made the whole thing unreliable.

This is probably the view that most Christians take.

There is a third position. In terms of the number of Christians worldwide, only a very small proportion would hold this sort of view but it is popular among Biblical scholars and it has therefore been highly influential in the study of the Gospels. It's called liberalism. Much of the research that has been done on the New Testament and on Mark is liberal, though by no means all of it.

Liberals note that the stories about Jesus were passed on by word of mouth before they were written down. The time when this happened is called the *oral period*. The oral period lasted for about thirty years, from Jesus' crucifixion until Mark wrote his Gospel. Liberals assume that the earliest Christians were not really interested in what happened. They were just interested in the message about their faith. The information about Jesus was not, they say, transmitted at all accurately during the oral period. The early Christians were not interested in historical accuracy and indeed had no interest in history at all.

Liberals argue that, as the Gospels are first century documents, the writers of these documents had very simple ideas. They were also superstitious: they believed in things like demons, angels, miracles and so on. So they added this picture of the world onto the genuine information about Jesus. They didn't distinguish between reality and fable. If it worked for the message, fine. We have to update the Gospel to make it relevant to modern human beings, not rely on age-old superstitions.

Liberals would say we now know very little about what Jesus was *actually* like. The Gospels are written to persuade people to follow Christianity, not to record history.

Mark's Gospel is not important because it describes what happened. It's important because of the message that it contains. It doesn't matter that Mark gets so much so very wrong. And so the question, 'What does it mean?' is more important than the question, 'Did it happen?'

Some liberals would go so far as to say that we know so little about Jesus that Mark isn't really important at all. We must just try to live as God would want us, by being kind to other people.

It has to be said that underlying the liberal position are a great many assumptions. We have already seen that oral transmission is *not* necessarily inaccurate, despite what the liberals assume. It was the standard way in the first century of retaining information. The idea that the evangelists were not interested in history is rather silly. History was not invented in the last hundred years; there were plenty of historians in the first century and Luke, for example, seems deliberately to be using the methods of a first century historian. People in Jesus' time were no more stupid than we are and they knew the difference between something that had happened and something that hadn't. And the view that angels, miracles and so forth are simply superstition – well, that's another big assumption. Whether miracles are possible is something that philosophers can examine and many Biblical scholars accept that they are possible. It's a huge leap into the dark simply to write them off altogether.

Liberals range from people who think like this to those who would say, for example, that Mark does have a lot of accurate information. We can trust his overall picture of Jesus, even if we can't rely on every single detail. Perhaps Jesus did not do all the miracles, say, but his message about love for others is still important.

If you think about these views of the Bible – fundamentalist, liberal and conservative – as a *spectrum* of opinion, it becomes clear that there are shades within these views. Not all conservatives or liberals would agree with other conservatives or liberals; some conservatives are more towards the liberal end of things than others.

14

Some liberals spiral off the scale so that their position, in all charity, is no longer really a Christian one. And from a fundamentalist perspective, anyone who disagrees is too liberal. Moreover, it's not very easy to match 'conservative', 'fundamentalist' or 'liberal' to the different Churches. There are conservatives, liberals and fundamentalists in nearly all the main Christian denominations. There are liberal Anglicans, conservative Anglicans, fundamentalist Anglicans; liberal Methodists, conservative Methodists, fundamentalist Methodists... and so on. It's worth noting, too, that Biblical fundamentalists tend to be found in the Protestant Churches, and that Roman Catholics tend to be conservative but not fundamentalist.

Much of this isn't easy. It raises big questions and people unfamiliar with the controversy can be quite alarmed that things they've always taken to be true can be assumed by others to be not much more than fables. Yet it's important to *try* to get things right, even if it's not easy.

After all, if the Bible is in some sense the Word of God, then it is absolutely vital to understand it properly. In the past, the Bible has been used to justify racism, sexism, wars of conquest and tyranny (none of which, of course, it *actually* supports). St Augustine (354 – 430 AD) suggested a rule for how people should interpret the Bible. It is based on Mark 12.28-34, which goes like this:

> One of the teachers of the law came and heard them debating. Noticing that Jesus had given them a good answer, he asked him, 'Of all the commandments, which is the most important?
>
> 'The most important one,' answered Jesus, 'is this: "Hear, O Israel, the Lord our God, the Lord is one. Love the Lord your God with all your heart and with all your soul and with all your mind and with all your strength." The second is this: "Love your neighbour as yourself." There is no commandment greater than these.'
>
> 'Well said, teacher,' the man replied. 'You are right in saying that God is one and there is no other but him. To love him with all your heart, with all your understanding and with all your strength, and to love your neighbour as yourself is more important than all burnt offerings and sacrifices.'
>
> When Jesus saw that he had answered wisely, he said to him, 'You are not far from the Kingdom of God.' And from then on no-one dared ask him any more questions.

Augustine said that any Christian interpretation of the Bible should build up both love of God and love of neighbour.

Suppose we apply this to today. Parts of the Old Testament support the idea of a holy war. The Old Testament says God frequently wanted the Israelites to butcher their enemies, including the children (see Joshua 6.15-21, for example).

Would it really help people to love God or their neighbour if they had to believe, as a fundamentalist might say, that this really happened?

Or suppose we take the radical liberal view that Jesus is an obscure historical figure about whom we can know virtually nothing. Would that help people to love God?

As is usually the case, the truth seems to lie somewhere between the two extremes. The ultra liberal view makes so many assumptions – such as saying that first century people didn't know the difference between something that happened and something that didn't – that it's hard to maintain. Fundamentalism means denying a great deal of what the sciences tell us about the world and about human beings; and trying to hold that every single word of the Bible is absolutely true means you have to tie yourself in knots to try to make everything fit together. The position this book takes is that Mark's account is essentially accurate. There may be details that are not historically correct, but Mark's overall picture can be trusted.

Day 1

Mark 1.1-8: The beginning of the Gospel

Books in the ancient world were generally called by their opening words, so the original name for Mark's Gospel would have been something like 'Beginning of the Gospel'. Mark states that the book that's about to be read is a message, good news, and that it's about Jesus Christ. (In fact, 'Jesus Christ' as a name for Jesus isn't a form used very often by the evangelists, though it's frequent in Paul. The words 'Son of God' are not in all the Greek manuscripts and may have been added later – though because the Greek expression used here isn't the usual way of writing 'Son of God' in that language, it may well be original.)

Mark does not have the birth stories of Jesus. Whether he knew them or not, we simply do not know. If he did, he never refers to them.

Instead, he starts immediately with John the Baptist.

The Jews believed that Elijah, the greatest prophet of the Old Testament, would return to herald the coming of the Messiah. This idea was based on Malachi 3.22:

> Behold, I will send you Elijah the prophet before the great and terrible day of the Lord comes.

It's interesting that in English Bibles, this is actually in the final paragraph of the Old Testament. It provides a suitable transition between the Old Testament and the New.

The version Mark quotes actually combines Isaiah (40.3) and Malachi 3.1 with Isaiah 40.3. It may be that the two texts were linked by early Christians, before Mark himself used them, to describe John's role.

Although Elijah may not literally have returned, there's a real sense for Mark that John *is* Elijah. What he wears – clothes made from camel hair and a leather belt – is exactly what Elijah wore (2 Kings 1.8). So, if 'Elijah' is back, the Messiah must be following close behind.

It seems likely that one of the objections some Jews had to Jesus was that he couldn't be the Messiah because there was no sign of Elijah. The answer to that was to say that John fulfilled Elijah's role.

John's baptism is not the same as Christian baptism; indeed, any ritual that involves washing can be called a 'baptism'. The baptism of

John, as it is called, had a different meaning: it showed people were cleaning up their lives, owning up to their wrongdoing, so they'd be ready to greet the Messiah when he arrived.

(Interesting that we know the Essenes used baptism and had a community in the desert. This may suggest that John had, at one time, been an Essene.)

John may be important, but he's not the most important person in Mark. As he says, 'After me, someone more powerful is coming. I am not good enough to get down and undo his sandals.' This was something a slave would do for his master every day; John says he is even less than the slave of the Messiah. And the baptism the Messiah will bring will be greater than John's: it will not be in water but in the Holy Spirit.

Exactly what that means is not really clear. John seems to be saying that Jesus will put people in touch with God in a way that he himself cannot achieve, though John seems to place a lot of stress on crisis and judgement. It's possible, too, that Mark's first readers, who had themselves been baptised, would have seen their own baptism as the baptism in the Holy Spirit – even if that was not John's original meaning.

John's Gospel says that some of Jesus' disciples were originally disciples of John the Baptist (John 1.35-42). Some scholars have suggested that Jesus himself started as a disciple of John. It's possible but there's no hard evidence. The idea may be surprising; surely Jesus would have had nothing to learn from John? But it's important to remember that Christians teach that, whatever else he was, Jesus was really and genuinely a human being – as human as you are or I am. Human beings learn and develop ideas. After describing the holy family's visit to Jerusalem when Jesus was twelve, Luke says, 'Jesus increased in wisdom and in stature, and in favour with God and man' (2.52). As a child, Jesus had human teachers; as an adult, presumably he learnt from others too. The idea that Jesus was once a disciple of John shouldn't be dismissed on the grounds that the Son of God couldn't possibly have learnt anything from any other religious teacher. If it's untrue, it's because of lack of firm evidence.

Son of God

One of the most important titles Mark uses for Jesus is 'Son of God'. The title appears in the first verse of the Gospel and Jesus is called 'my beloved Son' by the voice of God when he is baptised. What does it mean?

The Jews of Jesus' time looked back a thousand years to the time of their greatest king, David. They believed that God has promised David that one of his descendants would always be the king of Israel (2 Samuel 7). Every king of Israel was anointed with oil at his coronation, so he was known as 'the Anointed One'. The Hebrew word for 'the Anointed One' is 'Messiah'; the Greek is 'Christ'. Effectively, 'Messiah' and 'Christ' are synonyms for 'king'.

As time passed, the last of the kings to be descended from King David – the last Son of David, as the kings were called – died. The Jews looked for God to send them a new Anointed One, a new Messiah. This new Messiah would be even greater than David and he would make Israel great again.

The Messiah was the Son of David. Another title for the Davidic king was 'son of God'; it was as though God adopted the king as his son when the king was crowned. But it was an *adoption*: the relationship between God and the king was like that of father and son, but there was no sense in which they were equals – in contrast to the beliefs of Egypt, just down the road, where the king was himself a god.

As we read through the Gospel, however, we will notice that Jesus hardly ever uses the title of 'Son of God'. He does not deny being the Son of God but it is only other people who call him that.

Why is this?

One possible reason is that Jesus did not want people to get the wrong idea about what sort of a Messiah he was going to be. Jews like the Zealots were expecting the Messiah to be a warrior king, but Jesus thought of his path as one of suffering.

After Jesus' death and resurrection, however, the early Christians felt able to call Jesus the 'Son of God' quite openly. There was no longer any danger that the title would be misunderstood, or that Jesus would be made the leader of a rebellion against Rome.

To consider:

When someone is baptised in the Church of England, they're told, 'Do not be ashamed to confess the faith of Christ crucified.'

As a Christian, are there times when I am ashamed to do this – to stand up for my faith?

Day 2

Mark 1.9-13: The baptism and temptation

It is interesting to wonder what was going on in Jesus' mind and how he felt when he was baptised – but we simply do not know. Mark does not tell us and, while some people may wonder, it can't be any more than speculation.

There are two common misunderstandings of this passage. One is that it was at this point that Jesus knew who he really was and realised his destiny. Mark does not say this and the other evangelists would say that Jesus was aware of his status well before he was baptised (see, for example, what the boy Jesus says to his parents in Luke 2.49). The second misunderstanding is to say that it was at this point that Jesus *became* the Son of God. This isn't at all what Christianity teaches. In fact, it's an old heresy called adoptionism: the idea that the human Jesus at some stage in his life *became* divine or achieved some sort of godly status. Christianity says that the man Jesus always was the Son of God; it wasn't something he only attained later (see, for example, Luke 1.35, John 1.14).

There are three points Mark is making:

1. The Kingdom of God is about to arrive. The Jews of Jesus' time were waiting for God to change history totally; to establish his rule on earth. Instead of human beings, *God* would be in direct control. They were looking forward, then, to the Kingdom of God. (There is more on the Kingdom of God on pages 37ff.)

2. The Holy Spirit has returned. The Jews in the First Century thought that the Spirit had spoken to the Old Testament prophets long ago. Since then, he had been very quiet, but many believed he would return with the Messiah. This is what happens. The Holy Spirit descends on Jesus 'like a dove'. Perhaps this is an echo of the story of creation in Genesis 1, where God's Spirit hovers over the unmade world. Or perhaps we could think of the dove which brought the olive branch to Noah, to show him the flood was over (Genesis 8.11). (Mark is not thinking of the dove as a symbol of peace; that's a later image.) Scholars have tried to work out why Mark says the Holy Spirit was 'as a dove', but nobody really knows. Moreover, while Luke's account takes 'as a dove' to mean the Spirit himself (3.22), Mark may mean that it was the *descent* of the Spirit that was dove-like: an adverb, not an adjective (the Holy Spirit descended 'dove-ily').

3. Jesus is the Son of God. This is the most important thing of all and it is announced by the voice of God. (Though notice Mark says *Jesus* saw the heavens opening; he doesn't say the others saw it. Presumably he thinks only Jesus heard the voice, too.) The words spoken by the voice come from one of the Old Testament Psalms, one which was used at the coronation of the kings of Israel:

> You are my son, today I have begotten you. (Psalm 2.7)

So Jesus is the King of Israel, the Messiah. Mark omits the words 'today I have begotten you'; Jesus does not *become* Son of God at this point; Mark is not an adoptionist. The voice confirms who Jesus already is.

The story has a darker side as well. The Old Testament book of Isaiah spoke of 'the Servant of the Lord'. Who the prophet originally meant by this is not clear, but the Servant goes on to die for the sins of the people. The early Christians identified the Servant with Jesus. The voice echoes what is said about the Servant in Isaiah 42.1:

> This is my servant, whom I strengthen:
> My chosen one, with whom I am pleased.

By echoing this, less than a page into his Gospel, Mark is preparing his readers for the death of Jesus.

The account of Jesus' baptism raises problems for Christians today. Why did Jesus, who never sinned, need to be baptised by John? Does that mean that Christianity has got it wrong and that Jesus could in fact sin? And doesn't it make it look as though Jesus is lesser than John, rather than greater?

The usual answer to this is that Jesus was identifying with the people who were being baptised; showing his solidarity with them. Moreover, there was a Jewish belief that the Messiah would be anointed by Elijah himself. Well, it's John as Elijah, and Jesus is 'anointed' with water rather than oil, but it does fit the idea. The baptism is an anointing, so Jesus is the Messiah.

The temptation of Jesus

Mark tells this story very briefly. He may have known the fuller version, which appears in Matthew and Luke (Matthew 4.1-11, Luke 4.1-13). It is often thought that Jesus needed time to reflect on and pray about his coming work; that is why he goes into the desert for so long. Interesting that the Spirit, who has just descended on Jesus, 'immediately' drives him into the desert.

The fact that Jesus himself was tempted is an important point. Even the greatest man who ever lived was himself tempted to do the wrong thing. So, there is nothing bad in being tempted; it's giving in that's the problem. One early Christian writer put it like this:

> [Jesus] is not one who cannot feel sympathy for our weakness. On the contrary, we have a great High Priest who was tempted in every way that we are, but did not sin. (Hebrews 4.15)

Finally, there was a Jewish belief that when the Kingdom of God arrived, there would be a battle against the forces of evil. In his temptations, by confronting the Devil, Jesus begins that battle.

To consider:

Temptations affect everybody. Sometimes what we're tempted to do seems very enjoyable.
   Do I have favourite temptations? What can I do to combat them?

Day 3

Mark 1.16-39: The authority of Jesus

In this section, Jesus begins his ministry. The first thing he does is to call the fishermen to be his disciples.

It's often thought that a 'disciple' means a 'follower'. In fact, it originally meant 'someone who learns': a student, or a pupil. (Notice how many times Jesus is called 'Teacher' in Mark.) In Jesus' time, many Jewish teachers had students or disciples. They listened to their master's teaching, and tried to learn it by heart.

(This may suggest, incidentally, that the Gospels record Jesus' words rather more accurately than some liberal scholars suggest. Jesus was a Jewish teacher. He would have used some of his colleagues' techniques.)

Yet Jesus was different from most Jewish teachers: they waited until people decided to follow them but Jesus *calls* people to be his students. And Jewish teachers' disciples were well educated; Jesus chooses ordinary people.

Simon (Simon Peter), Andrew, James and John worked on the Sea of Galilee ('Lake Galilee' in some translations). The fishing industry was very important: most Galileans ate meat once a week at most and fish was the major source of protein. The Jewish historian Josephus says there were over 300 fishing boats of the Sea of Galilee in the First Century. It has also been suggested that Peter was a fisherman who was in charge of a small fleet. If so, Jesus chooses all kinds of working people as his disciples, not just the poorest.

When Jesus tells the four men to follow him, they do not hang about. They drop everything to start their new life. They will no longer catch fish, but people.

The story continues with Jesus teaching in the Capernaum synagogue. The Sabbath service consisted of prayers, a blessing, readings from the Jewish scriptures and a sermon. The sermon commented on the readings, and any adult male could be invited to preach, especially if he was skilled in explaining the Torah. So Jesus began to teach. Mark does not tell us here what Jesus said, but he does say that 'they were astonished at his teaching, for he taught them as one who had authority, and not as the scribes [taught]' (Mark 1.22).

Jesus showed his authority, too, by casting out evil spirits. The Jews believed that God had made the world, and that it was good (Genesis 1.1-2.4). But they also knew there was a lot of suffering. They believed that illness – especially mental illness – was caused by evil spirits. Mark thinks the demon knows who Jesus is because it has some kind of supernatural knowledge. It also knows that, with the arrival of the Messiah and of the Kingdom he brings, the demons' days are numbered.

Belief in demons or devils

There's nothing to say that Christians today have to believe in demons: some do, and some don't. Are there such things, or are they just hangovers from an age before science? It may help to consider what exactly people in Jesus' time believed about them.

Some said there were over seven million devils in the world, and they were very dangerous. Devils liked to live in tombs and places where there was no water, although they could be anywhere. They were most active at night and in the heat of midday, and were particularly dangerous to travellers, women giving birth, and children who were out after dark.

There were three main ideas about where they came from:
1. Some said they were the spirits of dead evil people.
2. Some said they had been around since the time when God created the world, and had tried to stop him from doing so.
3. Some said that when the world was young, two angels came down to earth because they loved women's beauty. (This story is based on Genesis 6.1-4.) One of them returned to God; the other did not. He had children: the demons.

Many, both Jew and Gentile, believed you could cast out or 'exorcise' demons, using spells and magic. Jesus does not use spells: he simply orders the demons to leave, and they do.

There was a general belief that when the Messiah arrived, he would destroy the demons. In Matthew's Gospel, Jesus says, 'If it is by the Spirit of God that I cast out demons, then the Kingdom of God has come upon you' (Matthew 12.28).

It's certainly difficult today to accept all the first century Jewish beliefs about demons. It's also clear that we'd have different explanations for a lot of the things they were said to do; a pre-scientific age attributed sickness and mental illness to demonic possession and we know it's not as simple as that. Whatever position we take, it's important not to throw the baby out with the bathwater. Evil is a reality and, whatever its origin, it must be fought.

Various cures (1.29-34)

The cure of Simon Peter's mother-in-law is rather different from the cure of the man with an evil spirit. Mark does not mention that Jesus *said* anything here; he simply touches her. There is no mention of a demon, either. If Mark thought the fever was caused by an evil spirit, he does not say so. Jesus, then, can deal with any form of illness, not just those caused by demons.

It is sometimes suggested that Peter himself is Mark's source for the story.

Mark believes Jesus often healed large numbers of people at once; he has two further accounts of this in 3.7-12 and 6.53-56. Like others in his day, Mark believes the demons have supernatural knowledge; here, they know perfectly well who Jesus is.

A preaching tour (1.35-39)

This section is pretty straightforward. Behind it seems to be the idea that Jesus did not want simply to be known as a miracle worker. He does care about people, but this is only part of the story. By including the words, 'They are all looking for you,' Mark seems to imply that everybody, then and now, is looking for Jesus.

The preaching tour is dealt with in just one verse, but it may well have taken months to carry out.

To consider:

What do I do to combat evil
   — in society
   — when I encounter it in my own life?

Day 4

Mark 1.40-2.12: Jesus heals a leper and a paralysed man

Leprosy is one of the oldest known diseases. It is caused by bacteria similar to those that cause tuberculosis, and is highly infectious. It attacks the nervous system, especially the nerves in the face, feet and hands. Pain cannot be felt in those areas, so victims can injure themselves without knowing it. It can be cured but leaves people mutilated if it is not treated.

The World Health Organisation estimates that there are nearly a million people with leprosy today. It is a disease that hits the poor, especially in Africa, Asia and Latin America.

In Jesus' day, the Jews were terrified of the disease, quite understandably. They were so worried about it that other skin diseases were classified as 'leprosy', and anyone who was thought to be a leper had to obey some strict laws. The Torah laid down the rules (Leviticus 13-14). If you were a leper, you were an outcast, outside God's chosen people. If you touched a leper, you were religiously unclean for a period: unfit to worship God. Lepers had to live alone. As they walked about, they had to shout the warning 'Unclean, unclean' to passers-by.

It is quite possible that the leper in this story had what we would today class as leprosy. Or he may have had one of the other skin conditions. Whatever is the case, he was an outcast – and we can imagine how that made him feel.

Both he and Jesus break the rules.

He goes straight up to Jesus, even though approaching someone like this was illegal. And Jesus actually touches him. By doing so, he risked infection and he made himself religiously unclean, but he puts the man's need first. He does not seem to think about himself at all.

It only takes a word from Jesus to cure the leper. Then Jesus follows the correct procedure and tells him to show himself to the priest. The Torah specified which sacrifices were needed once a priest had checked a leper was clean; after that, the leper would be welcomed back into society. Jesus, then, is interested in the care the leper receives after his cure, too.

The Messianic secret

At least nine times in Mark, Jesus forbids people to spread the news about him, or to say who he is. *It is as though the fact that Jesus is the*

Messiah is a secret he wants to keep, but which always leaks out. New Testament scholars call this theme in Mark the 'Messianic Secret'.

Why the Gospel has this theme at all is still debated. Several explanations have been suggested:

1. Jesus was not in fact the Messiah, and no-one who knew him ever thought he was, either. Later on, Mark, who believed Jesus *was* the Messiah, had to explain why nobody who met Jesus had ever noticed!

   To get round this problem, Mark came up with the idea of the Messianic Secret. A few people, Mark claimed, *did* believe Jesus was the Messiah, but they kept it quiet. That was why no-one appears to have noticed: only a few knew, and they kept their mouths shut. This explanation of the Messianic Secret was proposed by a German New Testament scholar, William Wrede, in 1901.

   Wrede's theory was once quite popular among liberal New Testament scholars. Few take it seriously now. If the theory were true, why does Mark keep saying that the news got out? It's clear Mark *didn't* think only a few people knew; the news about Jesus' identity, he makes clear, spread like wildfire. This was because, despite Jesus' instructions, people did not keep the secret. They spread it around instead.

2. Another, perhaps more likely, view takes Mark more seriously as a record of what actually happened. When Jesus was preaching, people had very different ideas about what the Messiah would be like. The Zealots thought he would drive the Romans from Israel. In Jesus' time, there was a very real danger that people would get the wrong idea about the sort of Messiah Jesus was going to be. To prevent this, Jesus tried to keep secret the fact that he was the Messiah. This may also be why he tends to call himself the 'Son of Man' instead.

3. There is a third idea, which can be combined with the first or second. The idea of a 'secret' was an important part of Jewish thought. Jewish writings often described God's plans as a 'secret', shared with very few people. Mark says that Jesus shared the secret with his disciples, or tried to. The time when the secret finally comes out for everyone to see is in the story of Jesus' death and resurrection. *The only time that Jesus clearly admits that he is the Messiah is when he is about to die* (see 14.62). The notice above Jesus' cross calls him the 'king of the Jews' (15.26): remember this is what the Messiah *was*. The Messiah will not kill other people: he

will be killed, and will rise again. Only when this happens will people understand what being the Messiah really means.

Jesus heals a paralysed man (2.1-12)

Making a hole in a roof and lowering somebody through it would have been quite easy: the roofs were made from beams, with branches between, plastered over with mud. The stairs were on the outside of the house. All that the men in the story had to do was to go up the stairs and break through the mud plaster. The damage to the house would have been easily repaired.

Jews in Jesus' time thought that disease or disability was caused by demons. Another idea was that sin sometimes caused illness. One rabbi from Jesus' time said:

> No sick man is healed of his sickness
> until all his sins have been forgiven him.

The paralysed man in Mark's story may have thought like this: he was disabled because God was angry with him. Jesus is trying to reassure him by telling him his sins are forgiven.

His words shocked some teachers of the Law or scribes. Jews believed that only God could forgive sins, so Jesus must be blaspheming.

Jesus understands why the scribes are worried. He tries to show them that what he has said to the paralysed man really is true. 'Look,' he says to them, 'is it easier to say, "Yours sins are forgiven", or to say, "Get up, pick up your mat and walk"?' (Remember that to the Jews these meant more or less the same thing.) To make sure that the scribes have got the point – that the Son of Man has authority to forgive sins – he repeats these words, and the paralytic gets up and walks.

Jesus is not just a wonder worker who cures people; he does what God does: he forgives sins. And as early as chapter 2, Mark introduces the conflict between Jesus and the Jewish authorities which will eventually lead to his death.

To consider:

Lots of Christians pay lip service to the idea that Jesus forgives sins but actually are very frightened that he won't forgive them. Do I accept Jesus' forgiveness?

The Son of Man

In the healing of the paralytic, Mark introduced a new title for Jesus: the Son of Man. Jesus seems to prefer calling himself this, rather than 'Messiah' or 'Son of God'. In fact, it is true to say that Jesus usually calls himself 'Son of Man'.

The title appears no less than fourteen times in Mark's Gospel. Only Jesus uses it; no one else does.

So, if Jesus called himself the Son of Man, what did he mean?

Unfortunately, we can't be absolutely certain. Scholars today still argue about precisely what Jesus meant. It's worth looking at their ideas, and thinking about how 'son of man' was used before the time of Jesus and how 'Son of Man' is used by Jesus, in Mark.

How was 'son of man' used before Jesus' time?

We can find the answer by looking at the Old Testament and other Jewish writings. (English Old Testaments sometimes translate 'son of man' as 'mortal man', 'a human being', or just 'man'. The Hebrew original always says 'son of man'.)

There are two ways in which the expression is used:

1. 'Son of man' can just mean nothing more than 'a human being'.

In Hebrew and Aramaic (the language Jesus spoke), 'son of man' can mean this (e.g. Numbers 23.19). It sometimes contrasts people's weakness with God's power. In the Book of Ezekiel, God calls the prophet 'son of man', which means just 'man' (e.g. Ezekiel 2.1).

If this is what Jesus had in mind, then when he calls himself 'the Son of Man', he just means 'this man here', or 'I'. (After all, a son of man would be a man, wouldn't he?) We could go through all the times when Jesus says 'son of man', and replace the term with 'I' or 'me'.

However, the idea that 'Son of Man' just means 'I' or 'a man' may be totally wrong. This is because:

2. 'Son of man' could also mean someone from heaven.

The prophet Daniel had a vision of 'someone like a son of man', who was given power by God (Daniel 7.13f).

Daniel is an example of apocalyptic literature; the word means 'to uncover or reveal secrets'. Apocalyptic literature usually describes God's victory over evil, judgement, and the end of the world. It uses very extreme and even grotesque imagery: word pictures of dragons, lakes of sulphur, monsters and so on act as symbols for events and people in the real world and how God will deal with them.

Daniel was written in the second century BC. Later apocalyptic books said the Son of Man was someone from heaven whom God would send to judge human beings. However, there are two major problems with these later apocalyptic books:

First, we do not know whether they thought the Son of Man was the same as the Messiah, or was someone else entirely.

Second, many scholars say that they were written after the time of Jesus. Others disagree. We do not know.

How did Jesus use the title of 'Son of Man'?

When you think about it, it's odd that Christians today call their founder Jesus *Christ*: Jesus the Messiah. Jesus himself hardly ever uses the term 'Christ'. Why? Why did he prefer 'Son of Man'?

As we have already seen, the Jews looked back to King David's time a thousand years before. David was the ideal king: heroic, generous, and a great man of God. But there was something else. He founded the first Jewish empire. Israel conquered other countries, and was a real world power – a huge contrast to its status in Jesus' time, when it was reduced to a second rate country incorporated into the Roman Empire. Surely, the Jews must have thought, if the New David, the Messiah, is coming, he'll make Israel great again. This would obviously mean a war with Rome: a war which the Jews would win, with the Messiah, the Son of David, to lead them into battle.

If all this is correct, then 'Messiah' or 'Christ' as a title carried too much baggage. Jesus would not have wanted people to get too excited at the idea that he was the Messiah, as they would think he was going to lead them into war against Rome. (Notice how cool Jesus' reaction is when Peter calls him the Messiah in Mark 8.29-30.) Perhaps better to avoid the whole issue, and call himself 'Son of Man' instead. This would be particularly true if Jesus used 'Son of Man' in the first way described above. Not a king, not a warrior, not another, greater David: just a person, just a man.

In Mark, Jesus uses the title to get across three key ideas:

1. The Son of Man has authority on earth.
2. The Son of Man must suffer, die, and rise again.
3. The Son of Man will return at the end of time.

Scholars argue over all this. Some say that only one or two of these three ways was actually used by Jesus. Others disagree. We can be sure, though, that *Mark* thought Jesus used the title to get across all three ideas, so let's look at each one in turn.

1. The Son of Man has authority on earth.
The Son of Man has authority on earth –
i. to forgive sins (2.10), and
ii. he is Lord of the Sabbath (2.28): he can change the Torah's rules about the Jewish holy day.

2. The Son of Man must suffer, die, and rise again.
This is the most important idea; most of the Son of Man sayings are about it.

In the Old Testament and apocalyptic books, there is no mention that this is the Son of Man's job. However, the book of the prophet Isaiah speaks of the Servant of the Lord. (Isaiah – the book – actually contains the words of at least two prophets: Isaiah himself, and a later, unnamed prophet. Because no-one knows what he was called, he's often referred to as Deutero-Isaiah. It's Deutero-Isaiah who wrote about the Servant of the Lord.)

No one knows exactly who Deutero-Isaiah meant by the Servant, but he does say that this figure must suffer and die for the sins of the people. It is not very likely that people before Jesus' time had made the link between the Servant and the Messiah. After all, the Servant of the Lord would suffer and die, whereas the New David would kill other people.

It is possible, though, that Jesus used ideas about the Servant when he talked about the Son of Man. For him, 'Son of Man' carried the baggage not of the Warrior Messiah, but of the Servant of the Lord. Even if this idea is incorrect, it does seem likely that *Mark* thought about the Servant when he records what Jesus said about the Son of Man.

(Mark 8.31, 9.9, 9.12, 9.31, 10.33, 10.45, 14.21, 14.41.)

3. The Son of Man will return at the end of time.
The Nicene Creed says Jesus 'will come again to judge the living and the dead'. Christians believe that Jesus will come back at the end of

time, wind up history, and judge everybody. The technical term given to this event is the *parousia*.

(Some more liberal Christians do not take this literally. They might say that we are judged by Jesus when we die, but that happens to us individually after the moment of death. Liberals might say that Jesus will not *literally* return at the end of time. This is simply imagery for the idea that Jesus will hold us responsible for the way we have lived.)

If you look up the verses in Mark which refer to the parousia, they seem to echo Daniel's vision, and possibly other apocalyptic books – if these were written before Jesus' time.

In the early twentieth century, scholars used to think that Jesus was talking about someone else when he said that the Son of Man would come to judge people. Very few of them now agree with this.

(Mark 8.38, 13.26, 14.62.)

It has to be said that most Christians probably misunderstand 'Son of Man'. Reading the Gospels, or hearing the Gospels in church, they'd recognise that Jesus is called both Son of God and Son of Man. They would then connect this with the doctrine that Jesus is fully God and fully human – and assume that 'Son of God' means that Jesus is fully God, and 'Son of Man' means that Jesus is fully human.

This isn't what either what Mark thought or what Jesus thought – although it correctly emphasises Jesus' humanity.

Day 5

Mark 2.13-22: The Messiah's Banquet

Jesus calls another disciple. This time, he calls a tax collector, not a fisherman.

We do not know who Levi's father Alphaeus was, but we do know something about Levi. It is almost certain that his other name was Matthew (which is what Matthew's Gospel calls him in its version of this passage). Levi's job was to collect taxes for the Romans. Galilee was an important place for trade, as merchants travelling from Africa to Europe usually made their way through the area. The government charged them a fee to use the roads, and Levi may well have collected this money.

Tax collectors were hated by almost everybody. They were paid by taking more money than the government needed, keeping the rest for themselves. Many became extremely rich at the expense of their fellow-Jews. They were thought of as outcasts, outside God's chosen people because of their reputation, because they often worked on the Sabbath, and because they had contact with Gentiles. So they were ritually unclean: unfit to worship God.

Jesus' call of Levi was very shocking. Jesus does not condemn him or avoid him but chooses him as a disciple. Like the four fishermen, Levi 'immediately' does what Jesus says.

Perhaps a modern equivalent of a first century tax collector would be a thuggish debt enforcer who worked for a loan shark. Levi and his ilk were not unfortunate people who were frowned on by snobs. They were genuinely nasty pieces of work. And yet it's one of them who Jesus calls to follow him. No-one is too bad to be saved.

Even worse, from the Pharisees' point of view, Jesus has dinner with Levi and other outcasts or 'sinners'. They too were ritually unclean. Some or all may have been people like tax collectors or prostitutes. Or they may have been what the Pharisees called 'the people of the land': those who lived in Israel but did not keep the Torah. One reason why devout Jews could not eat with them was that they did not prepare their food in the ways the Torah set down. But there is room for them in God's new society, in his Kingdom.

The scribes – these ones were also Pharisees (verse 16) – did not like the idea of Jesus eating with such people.

Pharisees *were* interested in getting people to change their lifestyles for the better, to repent. But they had to keep the rules first. Jesus, by contrast, goes straight to the outcasts. He treats them with the same kindness he offered to everyone else. It's people like this who need him most. A doctor is needed more by people who are ill than by people who are well, after all.

(Jesus says, 'I have not come to call the righteous, but sinners.' It's possible that he means the 'righteous' are smug, self satisfied people and he is not here for them, but that is rather unlikely. 'Righteous' here probably means not the smug, but people who are in the right with God. So, if they're already right with God, Jesus needs to prioritise and to help the people who are not.)

The question about fasting (verses 18-22)

'Some people' – presumably the Pharisees again – ask Jesus why he and his disciples were not fasting. The Torah said:

> Man does not live by bread alone, but…by everything that proceeds out of the mouth of the Lord. Deuteronomy 8.3

So, for the Jews, the idea of fasting reminds them they do not just need food; they need God as well.

The Jews all fasted – they still do – on the Day of Atonement. On this Day, they remember their sins and fast to show they are serious about asking for God's forgiveness. Very strict Jews in Jesus' time also fasted every Monday and Thursday from 6 a.m. to 6 p.m. This may have been what the followers of John the Baptist and the Pharisees were doing.

Jesus was not against fasting; he was simply saying that now was not the right time. The Messiah was with them; it was time to celebrate – as you would at a wedding feast.

No-one would want to miss that. The bride and groom did not go away on honeymoon; they stayed at home for the party, and the party went on for a week. It was no time to be solemn, and no-one fasted while there was a wedding on. Indeed, one rabbi from around Jesus' time said the coming of the Messiah would be like a wedding.

The wedding celebrations stopped when the bridegroom left. 'The time will come,' says Jesus, 'when the bridegroom will be taken from them, and on that day they will fast.' Jesus is saying four things here:
1.   He is talking about who he is. In the Old Testament, God is sometimes called the 'bridegroom' or the 'husband' of the people of Israel (Isaiah 54.5 and 62.5) and his relationship with his people is like a marriage. In Mark, Jesus never directly says he is God made man, but he does take images about God and apply

them to himself. And Jesus does what God does (such as forgiving sins, which we looked at on Day 4). It's not very difficult, then, to work out the implications of all this.

2. He is talking about what he does. The 'marriage' between God and the people in the Old Testament is not stable; the people keep breaking their side of the agreement (covenant). The prophet Hosea said things had got so bad there had actually been a divorce. But Hosea also said there would be a new 'marriage' between God and the people. Jesus is the 'bridegroom' in this new 'marriage'.

3. He is saying what will happen to him. The bridegroom will be taken away; he will be killed by crucifixion.

4. He is saying what will happen to the bridegroom's friends. These are the Christians, and they will resume the practice of fasting after Jesus' death. The first Christians did this often; many Christians still do. For example, the holy days of Ash Wednesday and Good Friday are days for Roman Catholics of fasting and abstinence. Catholics are meant to fast from meat and abstain from alcohol on those days. Many Catholics fast from meat on Fridays, which is where the 'fish on Friday' tradition comes from. They're also meant to fast from everything except water for an hour before they receive communion at Mass. Christians generally may fast to prepare for special work, or to free themselves for an uninterrupted time of prayer.

The last two verses need unpacking:

'No-one sews a patch of unshrunk cloth on an old garment. If he does, the new piece will pull away from the old, making the tear worse.' If you have an old coat or garment, it's no good patching it with unshrunk cloth. When it shrinks, the patch will tear away from the hole and make things even worse.

'And no-one pours new wine into old wineskins. If he does, the wine will burst the skins, and both the wine and the wineskins will be ruined. No, he pours new wine into new wineskins.' Wine was kept in bags made from animal skin, which eventually became old and brittle. The gas from the fermentation stretched the wineskins. After a while, there was no more 'give' in the fabric, and they had to be thrown away. So new wine had to be poured into fresh, flexible wineskins.

Both images really get across the same idea: the old and the new don't and can't mix.

The new things are Jesus himself, and the rule or Kingdom of God which he brings. The old things are the ways the Jews have been living up to now. He is not saying the old ways are stupid and useless; Jesus was himself a Jew and he knew the Torah. But he is saying that it's now time for the old to make way for the new. And that made a lot of people very uncomfortable.

The Messianic Banquet

It was said in Jesus' time that the age of the Messiah would be like a huge dinner of celebration, a banquet. This image is in the background every time the Gospels say Jesus ate with people. So, when Jesus eats with the tax collectors and sinners, they're taking part in God's new society of the Kingdom of God. And another name for the Kingdom of God was the Messianic Banquet. The imagery of the Messianic banquet lay behind two ritual meals which the early Christians shared: the agape (pronounced 'aggerpay') and the Eucharist.

The agape was a meal, with prayers, which took place as an act of worship. We know very little of the details. There is some evidence that the early Eucharists formed part of this 'love feast' (which is what the word 'agape' means), though this is not certain. The agape is not very common today, though it is sometimes revived by modern Christians.

The Eucharist has been very important to Christians right from the beginning. For Orthodox, Roman Catholic, most Anglican and some Protestant Christians, it is at the heart of their worship. The Eucharist re-enacts the Last Supper but it also represents the Messianic Banquet.

To consider:

The Eucharist or the Lord's Supper is a representation of the Messianic Banquet.

The Kingdom of God

The Jews were once the leaders of a proud nation. They once had their own empire and their kings were adopted as his sons by God himself. They were a leading power in the world and the Old Testament told the story of their glory days, especially when they were ruled by King David.

But...

It hadn't been like that for a long, long time. For nearly six hundred years, the Jewish state had been passed around different world empires. And the Jews were sick to death of it.

For centuries, other countries had taken the Jews' freedom away from them. So they started looking forward to an age when they would have it back, for the time when *God* would be in charge. God would save them from their enemies, just as he had long ago saved them from the Egyptians. And this time, it would be final.

Instead of just another kingdom of human beings, the Kingdom of *God* would arrive.

The Jews' ideas about the Kingdom of God first grew up over 500 years before Jesus was born. Israel was at war with Babylonia (modern Iraq), and was losing. In 587 BC, the Babylonian army went on the rampage in Judah. Jerusalem was captured, buildings were demolished, the Temple was desecrated. Hundreds died. The survivors became prisoners of war in Babylon.

The prophets' writings from this period contrast the people's terrible suffering with a golden age, still in the future, but certain to come.

The Babylonians were later conquered by the Persians, who let the Jews go home. But the Persians were in charge, and the Jews were still not really free. The Persians' rule was followed by the Greeks', and then by the Romans'.

All this time, the people still longed for God to be in charge: for the coming of the Kingdom of God. During Jesus' lifetime and just before it, most Jews thought God was going to intervene and help them soon. The Kingdom would arrive quickly. (The Sadducees weren't all that bothered about this idea. Money and power were much more interesting.)

The technical term for ideas about the Kingdom of God is *eschatology*.

One of the main ideas people had about the Kingdom of God was that God would send the Messiah to lead them. We have seen that people in Jesus' time had different ideas about the Messiah. But they also had different views about what the Kingdom of God was going to be like. God was going to be in charge, but what would this mean?

The Zealots thought that if God was going to be in charge, the Jews would be in charge. They thought along secular and military lines. *God's* Kingdom was a *Jewish* Kingdom. The Son of David – the new, greater David – would rule the Kingdom of God on God's behalf. The Romans would be thrown out, and a Jewish empire would be born.

The Essenes emphasised the supernatural more. They believed that the Kingdom of God would begin with a battle against the forces of evil, both human and demonic. The Essenes did not think the Kingdom of God would be a Jewish empire. They believed it would be paradise: a new world which God had cleansed from evil. ('Evil' here also meant 'people who the Essenes didn't like'! A nastier kind of religion, both then and now, is to lump together everyone who dares to disagree with you as enemies of God.)

What did Jesus think about the Kingdom of God?

Mark says that Jesus taught the Kingdom of God was arriving. Indeed, the Kingdom of God was the heart of Jesus' whole message. The very first words Jesus says in Mark are in 1.14-15:

> After John was put in prison, Jesus went into Galilee, proclaiming the good news of God. 'The time has come,' he said. 'The Kingdom of God is near. Repent and believe the good news!'

Jesus said that the Kingdom of God was about to arrive. But he did not mean the same as the Zealots or the Essenes. So what *did* Jesus mean?

Jesus' view of the Kingdom in Mark.

1. God will bring it about.
Jesus disagreed with the Zealots when they said that the Kingdom could be brought near by fighting for it. *People* could not bring in the new age, *only God could.*

The Kingdom was like a seed growing into a plant. God makes the seed grow, and he makes the Kingdom come:

The Kingdom of God is as if a man should scatter seed upon the ground, and should sleep and rise night and day, and the seed should sprout and grow, he knows not how. The earth produces of itself, first the blade, then the ear, then the full grain in the ear. But when the grain is ripe, at once he puts in the sickle, because the harvest has come.

(Mark 4.26-29: the parable of the growing seed)

2. The coming of the Kingdom means a struggle.

If God is going to rule, then evil must be stopped. People's lives will be changed. Mark shows how he thought Jesus acted as though this struggle had already begun:

a) The Kingdom brings a struggle against sin, which Jesus forgives (2.1-12).

b) It brings a struggle against illness, which Jesus heals (e.g. 1.40-45, 5.25-34).

c) It brings a struggle against demons, which the Jews and Mark believed could possess people, and which Jesus overcomes (1.21-28, 5.1-20, 9.14-29.)

3. A new society will be born.

The Kingdom of God did not just mean the rule of God. It also meant *the people in the Kingdom*. The Jews were God's chosen race, yet Jesus taught that anybody could get into the Kingdom – including those who were excluded by mainstream Judaism from God's people: sinners, outcasts, and Gentiles.

This is summed up when Jesus said:

It is not the healthy who need a doctor, but the sick. I have not come to call the righteous, but sinners.   (Mark 2.17)

According to Mark, Jesus was on good terms with the Gentiles: he healed a Gentile madman (5.1-20) and a demon-possessed girl (7.24-30), and cured a Gentile who was deaf and hardly able to talk (7.31-37).

The people in the Kingdom of God – Jews, Gentiles, outcasts, righteous and sinners – would not only be members of the Kingdom until they died. Christianity teaches that you remain a member of the Kingdom after death as well.

How far does Mark's eschatology accurately reflect Jesus' eschatology? Biblical scholars disagree. Some of this disagreement reflects their own assumptions about the general accuracy of the Gospel documents, and we perhaps shouldn't be too worried by the fact that not all the experts say the same thing. (If you put four different biblical scholars in a room, you'll end up with five opinions.)

39

Over the past hundred years, there has been an enormous amount of discussion about Jesus' eschatology. A major reason for this is that, although the Gospels sometimes show him talking about the Kingdom of God *as though it had already arrived with his preaching*, at other times he spoke about it as though it was *still somehow in the future*. (Compare, for example, Mark 9.1 and 12.34.)

Some more liberal scholars think that Jesus really expected God to end the world and remake the universe. They say that he thought this would happen very quickly, perhaps within the lifetime of his own followers. If so, he thought about his work not as bringing in the Kingdom, but as preparing for its arrival.

Others disagree. They say that Jesus taught that the Kingdom had *begun in his preaching and ministry, but that at some time in the future it would be fulfilled.* This view considers the Gospel record to be more accurate than do rival views and it is, after all, the position of Mark himself. We adopt this position in this book, too.

To sum up:

We can say that everything Jesus says and does relates to the Kingdom of God:
— The parables teach about the nature of the Kingdom of God;
— The miracles are performed on different sorts of people, who become members of the Kingdom of God: children, women, outcasts, Gentiles;
— People who are members of the Kingdom have their sins forgiven by Jesus;
— If you become a member of the Kingdom now, your membership will continue after your death;
— Jesus' claims about himself are claims about the Messiah, who brings in the Kingdom of God;
— The arrival of the Kingdom means old fashioned ways of thinking are no longer important;
— Members of the Kingdom have to behave in a new way; at the heart of this is loving their neighbours as themselves (12.28-34).

Day 6

Mark 2.23-3.6: Rules, regulations and religion

Perhaps the nastiest rows are in families. There's something very upsetting about people who are very close falling out with each other. And the wounds can take a long time to heal.

The first Christians and Jesus himself were all Jews, and Christianity is a daughter religion of Judaism. Jews and Christians could be said to be part of one family. Sadly, that family has seen a lot of rows.

Some of this still continues. Yet today Christians and Jews co-operate on many projects and enjoy good relationships with each other. Pope John Paul II suggested that Christians should think of the Jews as their older brothers and sisters.

When Mark was writing, there had been a big falling out between Christians and Jews. Christians simply could not understand how the Jewish people could not see that Jesus was the Messiah they had been waiting for. Jews could not understand how Christians could say that, with the coming of Jesus, the Torah was no longer very important. The pages of Mark still ring with the sounds of the rows.

They're especially audible in the accounts of the arguments between Jesus and the Pharisees and scribes over the Sabbath. Mark includes them because he's interested in the question of whether Christians should still keep the Torah. To some extent, Mark makes Jesus' opponents represent the Jews with whom the Christians had fallen out. Some scholars suggest that this colours the way he presents his material. The Pharisees and scribes come across as being bigoted and heartless, which may be rather unfair. But the idea of respecting people who disagree with you is a modern one, not a first century one.

We now examine some material in Mark which deals with the Sabbath.

The Sabbath corn (2.23-28)

One of the ways the Law of Moses protected the poor was to allow them to pick food from growing fields or vineyards, as long as they did not use tools or carry large quantities away with them (Deuteronomy 23.24). So Jesus' disciples were not stealing; what made the Pharisees angry was that they were doing it on the Sabbath.

The Pharisees believed that the most important thing in life was to obey the Law, the Torah. So they were very careful to avoid anything which might infringe the Law, even in the smallest way, and they expected others to do the same. They had their own ways of interpreting the Torah which helped them to obey it, and they often added rules of their own, to prevent them breaking it by accident. They called this 'putting a fence around the Law'.

The Pharisees in Mark's story probably thought that Jesus' disciples were breaking the part of the Law which said that you should not reap on the Sabbath, even during harvest time (Exodus 34.21).

Jesus' answer shows a different way of thinking altogether. As far as he is concerned, people come first: the Law is given to help them. That is why Jesus reminds the Pharisees of the Old Testament story about King David. He broke the Law when he was hungry, just as the disciples do.

Finally, Jesus drops a bombshell. 'The Sabbath,' he says, 'was made for the good of human beings; they were not made for the Sabbath.' Jesus claims the authority, as the Son of Man, to have the last word on what may or may not be done on the Sabbath.

The man with the paralysed hand (3.1-6)

Mark makes it clear by this time everyone was agreed that Jesus could perform miracles. Nobody in the story seems surprised that the man is healed. The big question now is not whether Jesus can heal people, but whether he does it on the Sabbath, in front of the Pharisees who are out to get him.

The 'people...who wanted to accuse Jesus of doing wrong' (verse 2) are the same as the Pharisees who left the synagogue at the end of the story. They may have been members of the Sanhedrin, important people. If so, they would have had seats right at the front of the synagogue, with a good view of everything that was going on. Despite this, Jesus tells the man to come up, and he heals him in front of them all.

This was a deliberate challenge to the Pharisees.

The Jewish laws about healing on the Sabbath were clear: it was allowed if somebody's life was in danger. But the life of the man in the story is not threatened. It may be unpleasant to have a withered arm, but it does not kill you. Jesus could easily have avoided upsetting the Pharisees by waiting until the next day before healing him.

Once again, Jesus puts human need above religious rules.

Moreover, the coming of the Kingdom of God changes everything. The Pharisees refuse to see this (verse 5) and are clinging to the old ways of thinking. But God's salvation is here. Even when a man is healed in front of them, the Pharisees only worry about rules. It is this refusal to accept the arrival of the Kingdom that leads them first to hate, and finally to plot to kill, Jesus (verse 6).

Note:

2.26: Mark's version of Jesus' words says that *Abiathar* was the High Priest at the time of the story about David, but Mark seems here to have made a mistake. The original story is in 1 Samuel 21.1-6, and the priest there is Abiathar's father, Ahimelech.

The regulations about the 'bread offered to God' (it is usually called the *showbread*) are in Exodus 25.30 and Leviticus 24.9.

The Herodians: Mark says that the Pharisees 'met at once with some Herodians'. It seems likely that they were the supporters of Herod Antipas, the ruler of Galilee, but we know absolutely nothing more about them. Mark is showing that a number of different groups were against Jesus. The Pharisees did not think very much of Herod. If they were willing to do a deal with his followers, they must have been getting very anxious.

To consider:

Human need is more important than religious regulations.

Day 7

Mark 3.7-35: 'Who are my mother and my brothers?'

It's easiest to divide today's text into two sections: the crowd on the seashore and the choosing of the twelve (3.7-19) and the story about Jesus and his family (3.20-35). Let's consider them separately.

The crowd on the seashore and the choosing of the twelve (3.7-19)

Mark gives another summary of Jesus' healing miracles. Here, people come to Jesus from all over Israel – and from Tyre and Sidon, two Gentile towns. This again shows that Gentiles were welcome in the Kingdom of God.

In the story of Jesus choosing the twelve, Mark notes that they were designated 'apostles'. This means 'ambassadors' – people who are sent. They are to do three things:
1. Be with Jesus. They are his close friends, and listen to what he says.
2. Preach. They are to spread the good news about the coming of God's rule, the Kingdom of God. These two points are the responsibilities of Christians today, too.
3. Drive out demons. They share Jesus' authority to heal. The Acts of the Apostles shows them performing miracles (for example, Acts 3.1-9).

Why *twelve*? Why not ten or eleven?

It needs to be understood that Jesus is founding a new people of God: the citizens of God's Kingdom. The Jews were divided into *twelve* tribes, named after the sons of Jacob, whose story is recorded in the book of Genesis. The *new* Israel, the new people of God, does not have twelve tribes, but it does have twelve apostles.

Jesus and his family (3.20-35)

It's pretty clear that Jesus' family get it wrong, but what they do is perfectly understandable. Many of them would have remembered Jesus as a toddler, as a small child learning to read and write, as a teenager, or when he worked as a craftsman. And now, people are saying he's the Messiah. He must be ill; he's deluded, surely?

It's hard to be certain, but it does look as though there's some jealousy here. It isn't easy to be the brother or sister of someone

44

who's famous or more successful than you. You can either rise above it, or give in to resentment and bitterness, and try to belittle the relative who's done well for himself. Perhaps this is what's happening in Mark's story. They know Jesus isn't really mad, but it makes them feel better to kid themselves that he is.

Jesus doesn't reject family values. (We can see this is the case by looking at Mark 7.1-13 and 10.19.) But the family is not everything. And you don't have to be a blood relative of Jesus to be in his family:

Anyone who does the will of God,
that person is my brother and sister and mother. (3.35)

The other accusation Jesus faces is much nastier. He's not ill, he's evil. The only reason he can cast out demons is that he's possessed by the prince of demons.

'Beelzebul' or 'Beelzebub' was the name of a god of the Philistines in Old Testament times (2 Kings 1.2). It means 'Lord of the Flies'. By Mark's time, it had probably become just another name for the Devil.

Jesus has two responses to the scribes' accusation. In the first place, it's daft. If the devils were fighting among themselves, they're finished. On the contrary, the 'strong man', the Devil, is paralysed – he's tied up. Jesus' miracles do not show he's possessed; there's a contest going on between good and evil, and evil is losing.

The second thing Jesus says is more complex. He says that *any* sin, blasphemy, evil action, viciousness, unkindness – anything at all – can be forgiven by God. Except for one thing: blasphemy against the Holy Spirit.

What does Jesus mean?

If you read the passage again carefully, the answer becomes clearer.

Blasphemy against the Holy Spirit means being genuinely convinced that evil is good, and good is evil.

Jesus' miracles are acts of kindness, compassion and goodness. Yet the scribes in the story say they're evil. So, something that's on the side of God – any act of kindness, any mercy, any love – is evil.

The problem, Jesus is saying, with this sort of twisted thinking is that it can't be forgiven – because the people who think like that don't understand they *need* to be forgiven. They don't think they've done anything wrong. And until they realise it, they can't accept God's forgiveness.

There are examples in history of people who have convinced themselves that evil is good, and good is evil. Lots of people today genuinely think that racism is a good thing. Presumably, many child abusers don't believe they're doing anything wrong. In the early days of Nazi Germany, some of the propaganda posters read, 'Jesus Christ has come to us in the person of Adolf Hitler.' And research shows that lots of people who took part in the extermination of the Jews genuinely believed that murdering innocent people – including children – was morally right. Many of the killers called themselves Christians.

A final comment on this section. We live in an age where Christianity is often mocked and regarded as politically incorrect: stupid, outdated and only for idiots. Lots of people would rather make nasty jokes about religion than think about it seriously. You don't have to watch comedy programmes on TV for long before someone takes a swipe at religion. Some newspapers take it as a given that all religion is dangerous.

Christianity is not easy. Following Jesus is not easy. But then it never was. Even people who knew Jesus personally didn't believe in him: some thought he was insane, others thought he was a dangerous maniac. People today who find it hard to follow Jesus are in good company, because it was always like this.

Notes

It's interesting in this story that Mark doesn't say Joseph, Jesus' stepfather, was present. We don't know what happened to him. Christian tradition says he died before Jesus grew up, so Mary was a widow by this stage. This seems quite possible, but we cannot be certain.

There's a denominational difference in the way Christians today interpret the New Testament's mentions of Jesus' brothers and sisters. The Roman Catholic position is that Mary remained a virgin all her life. As a result, the 'brothers' and 'sisters' are said to be relatives of Jesus or 'brothers' and 'sisters' in a spiritual sense. Other denominations take the view that they were indeed Jesus' siblings – or half-siblings, to be more precise. The most obvious reading of Mark is that he took them to be Jesus' younger brothers and sisters.

Mark shows very little interest in Jesus' family. He doesn't tell the story of Jesus' birth, as Matthew and Luke do. Mary appears frequently in John's Gospel. Mark doesn't even call her by name here. Some scholars think this is because Mark, for some reason, was hostile towards the Church in Jerusalem, which was run by James the brother of Jesus (Acts 15.13, Galatians 2.9). Mark is having a go at them by saying Jesus' family were against Jesus. This may be right, but it's worth bearing in mind it's just a guess based on this story. Mark seems to be far harsher about Peter, who denied he even knew who Jesus was. Yet Mark is usually thought to be pro-Peter. Perhaps Mark is just being honest about the failings of James and the rest of Jesus' family, just as he was honest about Peter?

To consider:

Jesus is good, but it would be a mistake to say he's 'nice'. It could be said he's far from being 'nice' either to his family or to the scribes. Real goodness means standing up for what is right; it can mean being uncompromising. 'Niceness' can mean being so afraid to give offence that things that are utterly wrong are left unchallenged.

Day 8

Mark 4.1-20: The parable of the sower.

Parables were commonly used by the Jewish rabbis and we have many examples from the time of Jesus. What is unique about the parables of Jesus is that they all relate to the Kingdom of God.

Mark's view is that Jesus' parables also are 'riddles' (another meaning of the Greek *parabolê*) which 'those outside' the Kingdom find impossible to understand; their minds are so closed that they cannot grasp the meanings:

> When he was alone, the Twelve and the others around him asked him about the parables. He told them, 'The secret of the Kingdom of God has been given to you. But to those on the outside everything is said in parables, so that,
> ' "they may be ever seeing but never perceiving,
> and ever hearing but never understanding;
> otherwise they might turn and be forgiven!"'   Mark 4.10-12

The disciples have been given the 'secret of the Kingdom of God', but others are 'outside' the Kingdom. To describe these outsiders, Jesus quotes the prophet Isaiah's words (6.9-10) about the people of his own time. No matter what Isaiah did, they would not listen to him, and could not accept what God was offering them. Jesus is saying that some people are 'tuned in' to the Kingdom and will understand the parables, even if they have to have them explained. But others are so stubborn that not even the parables will help them. So *people's response to the parables is the same as their response to the Kingdom.*

The Parable of the Sower

The explanation of the parable in verses 13-20 seems a very good one. We all know people who lose their enthusiasm for something after a while, and who drop whatever it is they have begun. And we know people who, once they are convinced about a cause, go steadily on.

Almost all New Testament scholars, however, say that these verses were not said by Jesus at all. They think the explanations were added later, to help Christians who were going through hard times. Reasons given are:

— Some of the words used in these verses are different from the ones

Jesus normally uses. For instance, Jesus does not talk about 'the word' in this way anywhere else, but we do find this expression in the writings of later Christian teachers.

– A parable usually only makes *one* point, but here we have a series of pictures about different things which happen to different types of people. Would anyone listening to Jesus have been able to understand all of them at once?

– Some of the things mentioned in the explanation sound more like what was happening in Mark's time rather than in Jesus' time. (One example is 'trouble and persecution' in verse 17.)

– The explanation does not really work; it's confused. Is the seed the word (verse 14) or the people who hear it (verse 18)? The meaning changes.

Mark thinks, then, that the sower is a type of parable called an *allegory*. In an allegory, every point of the story represents something else and the explanation can be very complex. Another allegory in Mark is the parable of the vineyard (12.1-12).

Most scholars say the explanation of the parable was not given by Jesus. Mark or someone before him has created it but that is *not* the same as saying it has no value. (Paul's letters were not written by Jesus but what Paul says is of considerable importance. The explanation may be inauthentic to Jesus but it has the authority of a New Testament writer, perhaps Mark, behind it.)

If all this is correct, what did Jesus *originally* mean by the parable of the sower?

Probably this:

Jesus is saying that the Kingdom will certainly come, despite its small beginnings in his own ministry and all the difficulties ahead. God is like a farmer sowing seed. He broadcasts it everywhere. Some finds good soil. Some falls on stony ground and some is choked by weeds. But the farmer knows the harvest will come. The followers of Jesus should not despair. Even when things seem to be going wrong, the Kingdom of God is coming.

To consider:

Are there things in the teaching of Jesus which my mind is closed against?

Day 9

Mark 4.21-34: The parables of the Kingdom

Mark himself is probably responsible for collecting these parables together; it is likely that Jesus originally taught them at different times. We'll consider each one separately.

A lamp under a bowl (4.21-23)

People use lamps to light a room, not to stick under a bowl or a bed. Jesus is saying that whatever is hidden will be brought out into the open. This general meaning applies to the Kingdom itself, and to its members:

Even if the Kingdom of God is difficult to recognise at the moment, Jesus' followers will see it. The disciples may have thought Jesus' message had not converted as many people as it should, yet the Kingdom is indeed on its way.

And the truth about Jesus and the Kingdom should not be hidden away. Those who believe in Jesus should not hide away the Good News; they should spread it. Those who are members of the Kingdom of God should not keep the Gospel to themselves.

'Those who have something will be given more' (4.24-25)

Translations of verse 24 generally try to make sense of something that looks very odd in the Greek. What Mark actually wrote was this:

And he said to them, 'See and understand. The measure you measure out will be measured out to you, and more will be given to you.'

This could mean any one of three things:
1. After their death, Jesus will judge people in the same way that they have judged others. This is how the Good News Bible understands it. Matthew and Luke have similar sayings which are talking about judgement (Matthew 7.2, Luke 6.38).
2. Or could just be saying something about life: we get out what we put in. If we put in a great deal, we may find we get even more from it than we expected. The problem with this explanation is that it does not relate to the Kingdom of God.
3. The probable meaning is that if people are tuned in to the Kingdom – if it really matters to them – their understanding of Jesus'

message will increase. Their faith and commitment will grow.

Verse 25 is translated by the NIV as follows:

> Whoever has will be given more; whoever does not have, even what he
> has will be taken from him.

Again, it is not very clear what this means. Jesus seems to be saying that if you are alive to God, the parables will make you understand things even better. If you close your mind to the Kingdom, the parables will just confuse you and make you worse off than you were in the first place. This might well apply to the Pharisees: they start off by not listening to what Jesus says, and end up by plotting to kill him.

The parable of the growing seed (4.26-29)

This is the second of the *parables of growth*: the first was the sower, and the next it the mustard seed.

New Testament scholars used to think that these parables showed that the coming of the Kingdom happened gradually: it takes time for a seed to develop into a plant, and it takes time for the Kingdom finally to arrive. However, this really misses the point. The important thing is that plants (which represent the Kingdom) do appear; how long they take does not really matter.

In the parable, the farmer leaves the seed alone once he has planted it. There are two possible ways of understanding this:
1. The farmer represents God. Just as the farmer allows the seed to get on with its job of growing, and gets on with his normal life, God lets the world run on normally, and then brings in the Kingdom (the harvest).

There are two problems with this view:
i) Many scholars think that when Jesus uses parables of growth, the plant, not the harvest, represents the Kingdom. The harvest represents the Day of Judgement, when people will have to answer to God for the way they have lived their lives.
ii) The Jews of Jesus' time just did not believe that God 'lets the world run on'. They thought that God was very active in what happened on earth.

A better idea seems to be:
2. The farmer represents the followers of Jesus. His job is to sow the seed, then it is left to the soil. The disciples spread the message, but they should leave it to God to bring in the Kingdom. Remember

the Zealots thought they could force it to arrive by fighting the Romans. Once more, Jesus shows that God's actions, not people's, make the Kingdom come.

The parable of the mustard seed (4.30-32)

Mustard plants can grow to a height of nine feet, even though they started life as tiny seeds. Jesus' work may seem to have little effect at the moment, but the Kingdom will come as surely as a mustard seed grows into a mustard plant.

In the Old Testament, world empires were sometimes described as trees which provide shelter for birds. The birds represent foreign nations who were part of an empire (Daniel 4.10-12). God's empire – the Kingdom – is a tree, and birds make their nests in it. Here, too, the birds represent foreigners. One Hebrew word, and one Greek word, is used for both 'foreigners' and 'Gentiles' – so the Kingdom of God includes Gentiles.

The mustard seed was not literally 'the smallest seed in the world'; this was a figure of speech used be people in Jesus' day. Mark actually says that the mustard plant us the biggest of all garden shrubs, not the biggest of all plants.

Why Jesus uses parables (Mark 4.33-34)

Mark mentions 'other parables' which he has omitted; this clearly shows he's making a selection; some of these other parables are found in the other Gospels. Mark says Jesus 'told them as much as they could understand'. Like any good teacher, Jesus made sure his pupils could understand what he said.

To consider:

If I'm a member of the Kingdom of God, what are my responsibilities
– to my fellow-members of the Kingdom,
– and to 'those outside'?

Day 10

Some scholars classify this story as one of the 'nature miracles', so called because Jesus behaves like God in using his power over nature. Other nature miracles are the feedings of the 5000 and the 4000, the walking on the water, and the cursing of the fig tree.

This is a modern distinction. Mark didn't think in terms of 'nature miracles', 'healings', 'exorcisms' or any other categories we might come up with. One reason we know this is because Mark says Jesus 'commanded' the storm, and the same word is used earlier to describe how he silenced a demon (Mark 1.25). Perhaps Mark thought that the storm was almost demonic. In any case, Mark thinks that miracles are miracles, and human suffering should be fought, whether it's caused by the forces of evil, by illness, or by natural disasters.

It's generally thought that Mark's Church was among the persecuted Christians in Rome in AD 64. If this is right, or if his readers were from some other persecuted Church, it may be that Mark had them in mind. Like the disciples, their lives were threatened, but they should trust Jesus ultimately to save them – even if they have to pass through death.

The account ends on a cliff-hanger: 'Who is this man?' As we've said before, Mark doesn't directly say that Jesus is God made man, but it's clear that he accepted the divinity of Jesus. Here, the language used is meant to lead his readers to this conclusion.

Anyone who read the Old Testament would know that it is God who has power over water: the spirit of God hovered over the waters of chaos when he created the world (Genesis 1.2), and God parted the Red Sea when the Jews were brought out of Egypt. There's an even clearer parallel with Psalm 107, which says that sailors in trouble –

called to the LORD
and he saved them from their distress.
he calmed the raging storm,
and the waves became quiet.   Psalm 107.28-29

It's pretty clear, then, what Mark's getting at!

Moreover, the disciples are 'afraid'. In the story, this isn't surprising: drowning isn't fun. But 'fear' in the Old Testament is generally the appropriate reaction to a theophany, a manifestation of

God. (For example, when he gave the Ten Commandments to Moses, the people 'trembled with fear' at the signs of God appearing on the mountain (Exodus 20.1-21).

'Who is this man?' Mark expects his readers to supply the answer.

It's sometimes said that the details given in this story – the mention of 'other boats' and the graphic detail that Jesus was sleeping in the stern, with his head on a pillow – are evidence of an eyewitness source, perhaps Peter himself.

To consider:

'Who is this man? Even the winds and the waves obey him.'

Day 11

Mark 5.1-20: The demoniac in the tombs

We've come across exorcisms before; the difference is that this one is on a much greater scale. This demoniac is not possessed by one demon; he's got a whole legion of them: the same number of devils as there were soldiers in a Roman legion: up to 6000. Mark shows they are no match for Jesus; even up against thousands of devils at once, Jesus just tells them to get out, and they obey him.

The herd of pigs locates the story in Gentile territory; the Torah forbids Jews to eat pork. This is confirmed by Mark's mentioning the Gentile region of the Decapolis (Greek for Ten Towns). Which precise town they were near is unclear. The territory of the Gerasenes was the area around Gerasa, over thirty miles from the Sea of Galilee. Other Greek manuscripts of Mark say they were in the area of Gadara. But that doesn't help much either, because Gadara's still six miles away, so the pigs would have had a long run. To be honest, it looks as though Mark's got muddled. He probably wrote that it happened near Gerasa, someone saw the problem and changed it to Gadara, which was better but still didn't really work. We have already noted that there are problems with Mark's geography.

Whatever the town is meant to be, it is clear that the demoniac is a Gentile. (Incidentally, he refers to God by a *Gentile* name: 'the Most High God' (cf Daniel 3.26)) Mark is once again making the point that Gentiles are included in the Kingdom. At the end of the account, the man preaches in the Decapolis about what Jesus has done; more Gentiles, as a result, would join the Kingdom.

In the first century, it was held that knowledge of someone's name gave you power over them. This is why Jesus asks the man his name, and could be why he addresses Jesus by name too. Tombs were believed to be favourite haunts for demons, who were thought to dislike leaving their chosen areas. And it was believed that demons could do something destructive when they were exorcised. The Jewish historian Josephus wrote about a demon upsetting a jug of water. Philostrates, a Greek writer, mentioned a demon who pushed a statue over. These are not as spectacular as a stampede of 2000 pigs, but they show us the sort of ideas Mark was used to.

Some Christians have no problem with this story: Mark, they would say, is reporting what actually happened. He had access to good sources (such as Peter himself) and the Holy Spirit prevented him from making any errors. For other Christians, the account is hard to take: it seems to rest on a lot of first century ideas like demons and exorcism, and what's said about the pigs seems very odd indeed.

This sort of book isn't really the place to stir up controversy. It's certainly true that most Christians for most of history have taken the story literally. More conservative Christians are unhappy with the idea that legendary material could be included in the Gospels. On the other hand, more liberal Christians can find this kind of account very difficult to accept, and to insist that it has to be taken as history does not help them. Whatever view we hold, it's probably best not to batter other people over the heads with it. It's uncharitable and it's probably best to agree to differ.

It's worth considering some ideas about this story's historicity, though – either to clarify our own thinking, or to help understand our fellow Christians' views.

One view is that this account is an old Jewish folk story, which has been altered so that it has become a story about Jesus. This is a guess; though there might have been such a tale, we certainly don't have a copy of it now.

A compromise position is that the miracle story (the cure) is authentic and it's been combined with a folk tale about the pigs. Or Jesus made the pigs stampede because it was the only way he could convince the man he had been cured, or they took fright when the man had a violent fit.

Whether we're dealing with legend or with history, in the context of the story, there are some aspects of the man's behaviour that support the view that he was severely mentally ill. (Some would argue this was actually his condition, which in the first century would have been understood as demon possession.) He self harms. He's been isolated from the rest of the community, who can't help with his extreme behaviour. He's delusional.

Today, our understanding of mental illness is much better than it was in the time of Christ. We no longer chain up schizophrenics or leave them to fend for themselves. There's a recognition that labelling the mentally ill as 'mad' isn't just simplistic but uncharitable as well; mental illness is common and there are a wide range of mental health problems, just as physical illness is common and has many varieties. Even so, there can be a tendency to say that only physical illness is *real* illness; the mentally ill – those who have depression, or who suffer from anxiety or bi-polar disorder – aren't really ill and should pull themselves together. The Churches are beginning to understand the needs of those with poor mental health, but there is still a very long way to go. Becoming better informed about the issues is a very good place to start.

To consider:

How much do I know about mental illness? Do I have colleagues or acquaintances who are in poor mental health? How much do I know of their needs – and can I help to meet those needs?

Day 12

Mark 5.21-43: Jairus' daughter
and the woman who touched Jesus' cloak

Both these miracles are about people who are beyond medical help.

Both are about females. This is significant, because women were very much second-class citizens. Jesus does not share this attitude. If someone is suffering, she or he must be helped. It makes no difference whether they are male or female.

The story about Jairus' daughter is interrupted by the healing of the woman who touched Jesus' cloak. It may have happened just as Mark reports it. But some note Mark's fondness for breaking up one story with another, even though they happened at different times. (For another example of this 'sandwich' arrangement, see 11.12-25.)

It is easiest for us to deal with each miracle in turn.

The woman who touched Jesus' cloak (25-34)

The woman suffered from a menstrual problem, or some kind of infection that produced similar symptoms. The bleeding had become a constant haemorrhage, making her weak and exhausted. It also made her ritually unclean according to the Torah: an untouchable, not allowed to worship as one of God's people (Leviticus 15.25). This had been going on for twelve years, and the doctors had been no help at all. But she has been told about Jesus' power to heal, and she has faith in him and in what he can do. 'If I just touch his clothes, I will be healed.'

Jesus somehow knew that 'power had gone out from him' and he wanted to know who had touched him. (The disciples, slow on the uptake again, think someone's barged into him.) The woman is clearly frightened but Jesus' reply is reassuring. In Greek, verse 34 says, 'Daughter, your faith has *saved* you.' Jesus cares not only for her physical health but for her spiritual well-being too. She can go in peace. Her faith in Jesus not only makes her well, it *saves* her. She is now one of the family – a 'daughter' of Jesus – and a member of the Kingdom of God.

Jairus' daughter (21-24 and 35-43)

Jairus was an official or 'ruler' of the local synagogue. This was really an administrative rôle: he made the arrangements for worship, rather than taking the services himself. Still, he was an important person in the community, and here, we have an example of a Jewish leader who was not against Jesus but wanted his help. He has complete faith in Jesus and in his power, even though his daughter is dying.

Jesus takes with him Peter, James and John: the three disciples who were often with him on important occasions (at the transfiguration, for instance, in Mark 9.2, and in Gethsemane, Mark 14.33). By the time they reach Jairus' house, the girl is dead, and the Jewish mourning ceremonies have begun. Even though he knows this, Jesus tells Jairus to have faith (to 'believe'). And then something absolutely incredible happens.

Jesus brings the dead girl back to life. The people who saw it were 'completely amazed'. And she was not a ghost or an illusion: she was walking around, and they gave her something to eat.

This story is very important to Mark because only God has power over death. In 1 Kings 17.17-24, the prophet Elijah prays that God will bring a boy back to life, and he does. Mark does not mention Jesus praying here: he himself brings the girl back from the dead. Jesus behaves as God behaves.

There is also a sense in which this story foreshadows the resurrection of Jesus. (There is a big difference, though. Jairus' daughter was brought back to *normal* life, and would die again. This is different from Jesus after his resurrection.)

It also underlines the idea that it is Jesus who grants life after death.

Mark reports Jesus' words in verse 41 as *Talitha koum*. This is not Greek, but Aramaic, the language Jesus spoke. Mark's Gentile readers may not have known Aramaic, so he explains what the words mean. It's been suggested that Mark may have had this detail from Peter, who remembered Jesus' original words.

To consider:

Jesus offers us life after death. Do we ever take this gift for granted?

Day 13

Mark 6.1-13: Faith: rejection and reception

In the previous stories of the calming of the storm, the demoniac in the tombs, Jairus' daughter, and the woman who touched Jesus' cloak, the idea of *faith* is important. Jesus rebuked his disciples for not having enough faith when they were on the lake; the demoniac wants to become a disciple when he's cured; Jairus and the woman have faith that Jesus can help them.

The theme of faith continues in this new story. Here, it's not that people have faith in Jesus, it's just the opposite. Jesus goes home, and the people in Nazareth can't accept him.

And Jesus' family thought he was out of his mind. Jesus meets the people he's known for years. They can't accept that the local carpenter's anything special. Presumably they've heard all kinds of rumours about him – but the rumours can't be true, can they? Everybody knows his family. Who does he think he is?

Jesus quotes a well known proverb to them: prophets are never recognised in their own towns. He's appalled by their lack of faith: they think they know him, but they don't.

It's important to realise that while there's no such verb in English as 'to faith', there is in Greek. It's usually translated into English as 'to believe'. When an English New Testament talks about people believing, it means 'having faith'.

Practically nobody at Nazareth is interested. Jesus now sends the disciples out to look further afield. His message was 'Repent, and have faith in the good news'; the disciples now spread that message more widely. Mark thinks the twelve are helping to bring in the Kingdom of God by sharing in what Jesus does.

He tells the apostles to travel light. They are to be completely dependent on God. Sandals and a stick are allowed, but no cash, bag, food or change of clothes. They must not stay anywhere too long, or waste time on people who won't listen. (The 'bag' here means the sort used by wandering preachers to collect cash. The disciples are not to take money from their audiences.)

The journey is urgent and important. Jesus tells the apostles that if they are not welcomed into a town, they must shake its dust off their feet when they leave. This is interesting, because it's what Jews did when they returned to Israel after being in a Gentile country. Dust from Gentile soil must not defile the Holy Land. But the people the apostles visit are *Jews*. Mark wants his readers to understand that times have changed with the apostles' journey. What matters now is not whether you're a Jew, but whether you accept the apostles' message about the Kingdom of God. By shaking the dust from their feet, the apostles warn people they could be left outside the Kingdom.

To consider:

Mark says Jesus could do little when people have little faith. Is my faith strong enough to enable Jesus to use me in his work?

Day 14

Mark 6.14-29: The death of John the Baptist

Mark tells this story so well that there is little that needs to be added to his account. We can note the following points:

- 'Herod' is Herod Antipas, the ruler of Galilee. He was answerable to the Romans, who gave him the title of *tetrarch* or ruler. Mark says he was a king, perhaps ironically: Herod was banished to Gaul for asking to be promoted to being a king.

- Marrying your brother's wife was forbidden by the Torah in Leviticus 18.16, 20.21. These verses are especially significant in English history, too: Catherine of Aragon, Henry VIII's first wife, was the widow of Henry's elder brother Arthur. When Henry wanted to marry Anne Boleyn, it was to these parts of Leviticus that Henry appealed. It was fine for him to annul the marriage to Catherine and to marry Anne instead: Catherine had been his brother's wife and Henry ought never to have married her in the first place. That's what Henry thought, anyway. As we know, he had a habit of getting his own way.

- It's not clear who Mark means by 'Philip'. Herod Antipas did have a half brother called Philip, but this Philip married Antipas's wife's daughter – who's *also* called Herodias in some manuscripts of Mark. Other manuscripts omit the daughter's name, which actually seems to have been Salome. Herodias (Antipas's wife, not stepdaughter) had been married to a different brother, who lived in Rome. Confused? Don't worry. Maybe Mark was as well. The Herod family had a habit of marrying each other's wives and often had very similar names. They also had a habit of murdering each other, but that's another story.

- The dance performed by Herod's stepdaughter was the kind of dance usually performed by a prostitute.

- It is highly likely that many people at the time thought John the Baptist was the Messiah. This may partly be why Mark spends so much space on John: he is trying to correct a wrong impression.

An account of John's death is also found in *Jewish Antiquities* by the Jewish historian Josephus. This is actually rather later than Mark's account; it was written in AD 93-4. It's interesting to compare the two. Here's what Josephus wrote:

Herod killed John, who was called the Baptist. John was a good man; he taught the Jews how to be virtuous – both in how they treated each other, and in worshipping God. He told them to come to be baptised… Many others came in crowds to him; they were greatly moved by his words. Herod feared that the huge influence John had over the people might lead him to organise a rebellion; the people seemed ready to do anything he told them. Herod put him to death. He thought this was the best thing to do, to prevent any mischief John might cause, and to avoid problems later…

Herod's suspicious temper led him to imprison John at the castle at Macherus. He [John] was executed there.

Jewish Antiquities (18, chapter 5).

To consider:

It's pretty clear from the account that Herod knew what was the right thing to do but did not have the courage to do it.
Is this ever true of me? If it is, do I pray for the courage to do what is right?

Day 15

Mark 6.30-44: The feeding of the 5000

It's pretty clear that this was a very important story for Mark because he tells it – or something very like it – twice. There's an account of Jesus feeding 4000 people in 8.1-10, which is usually taken to be a variant of this miracle.

Given that Mark's space was limited and that he had other material about Jesus which he could have included instead, why spend so much time on the stories of the miraculous feedings?

The answer seems to lie in the stories' symbolism. (This is not to say that they're unhistorical. An account of an historical incident can, after all, still be told because the author wants to convey other ideas to his readers.) It's generally thought that this is a Christological miracle: it's related to who Jesus is. Moreover, the meal itself symbolises the Messianic Banquet and looks forward to the Last Supper and the Eucharist. We'll consider these ideas in turn.

Who Jesus is

During the Exodus, the Torah says that God provided food miraculously for the Jews as they wandered in the desert: every morning, manna appeared on the ground.

Here, it is Jesus who miraculously gives people food in the desert. (In verse 32, the location of the incident is said to be a 'lonely place' – it varies in some translations – but this can also mean 'desert place' or 'wilderness'.) Once more, Jesus behaves as though he were God.

Jesus is also shown to be like Moses. One rabbi had said:

The first redeemer [Moses] made food come down from heaven.
The last Redeemer [the Messiah] will too.

Through Moses, God spoke to the people and told them how to live. In Jesus, Mark believes, God speaks to the people in a new and greater way.

There's a similar, though much less spectacular, feeding miracle in the Old Testament. In 2 Kings 4.42-44, the prophet Elisha fed a hundred men with twenty small loaves. There's a link, which sounds pretty convoluted, but which would have seemed much more straightforward to Mark's original readers. Elisha was the successor of Elijah. Elijah was going to return to prepare the way for the

Messiah. Jesus is like both Elisha (and therefore Elijah) and Moses. Therefore, it's as though both the Law (Moses) and the Prophets (Elisha) are fulfilled in Jesus.

The miracle looks forwards to the Last Supper and to the Eucharist

As we have said, all the meals in Mark are in part symbolic. People in Jesus' time said that the Kingdom of God would be like a celebration meal: the Messianic Banquet.

The feeding of the 5000 also foreshadows the Last Supper and the Eucharist. We can see this by the close similarities in Mark's wording of what Jesus did: in the miracle, Mark says:

> And taking the five loaves and the two fish he looked up to heaven, and blessed, and broke the loaves, and gave them to the disciples to set before the people...   (6.41)

– and at the Last Supper, he says:

> And as they were eating, he took bread, and blessed, and broke it, and gave it to them...   (14.22)

Took (or 'taking'), blessed, broke, gave. The parallels are clear. Jesus shares the bread with the crowd, and he will share the bread of his body with the disciples at the Last Supper, and with all Christians at the Eucharist.

(Incidentally, when it says Jesus 'blessed', it means he blessed God. He is acting as a typical Jewish host at a meal, thanking God for food before handing it out. He 'looked up to heaven' as a sign of thanks, not as a bit of mumbo-jumbo to make the miracle work.)

So three meals are told of in this story, one directly, two indirectly:
– Jesus saves people from their hunger (the feeding miracle)
– Jesus saves people from death by dying for them (the Eucharist)
– Jesus saves people from death to enjoy the Messianic Banquet of the Kingdom of God.

What really happened?

For some, this miracle is rather hard to take, and a number of explanations have been put forward. It has to be said that there's no real evidence for these explanations: all we have is the text, plus some speculation. Lying behind attempts to explain away the feeding miracles is an assumption – and that's all it is – that Jesus could not possibly have done anything like this.

To this, the answer is: well, why not? If we believe in God, we believe in someone who is omnipotent: so powerful that he can think an entire universe into existence. If that's the case, then making some extra rolls and fish is not exactly going to be much of a problem for him.

However, some of the explanations are quite widely known, so it's worth noting them.

It's been suggested that there is some exaggeration going on. In reality, it was only a few people who were fed, in which case there was enough food to go round. Or the crowd only received a tiny scrap of bread each. The problem with both these suggestions is how anyone could then have mistaken it for a miracle; it clearly wasn't.

Or it's suggested that the people in the crowd saw Jesus was willing to share his food with them, and they felt guilty. They shared their own food with each other. But again, why would anyone mistake this for a miracle? If I offer you a jaffa cake from my packed lunch, you might enjoy it, but you're unlikely to think it's a miracle.

There's also the bizarre suggestion that Mark's saying the people sat 'by hundreds and by fifties' shows that behind the story is actually a meeting between Jesus and a band of Zealots. This is because Zealots would form groups of a hundred or groups of fifty as part of their drill.

What exactly Jesus was doing with a battalion of Zealots is not explained. It seems rather unlikely that the Prince of Peace would want to associate with a bunch of terrorists. Moreover, this 'explanation' says that the historical core is such a meeting – but the account as a whole reads nothing like that.

Well. Knowing something about the history of biblical scholarship may help us understand what's lying behind these explanations. In the Victorian period, the early liberal scholars decided that miracles could not possible happen, and came up with rather unconvincing reconstructions of what really happened. So, when the storm stopped it was just a coincidence; Jesus was not walking on the water but on some stepping stones; the child was not dead but sleeping; and so on. It could be said that it's rather more difficult to believe in these 'explanations' than it is to believe in the miracles themselves. The 'explanations' for the feeding of the 5000 look rather like hangovers from this sort of thinking.

More modern liberal biblical scholars very rarely propose these sort of theories. They tend to assume that the miracles did not happen, but the explanation is that they're purely literary creations. To put it less politely: they're made up stories.

Again: assuming that Jesus did not perform miracles is a presupposition. If we believe in a closed universe, or that God would be unjust to help some people in distress when he does not save all of them, then it would follow that the miracles of Jesus are unhistorical. But if we start with the records of the Gospels themselves, there is so much emphasis on the miraculous that it has to be asked: if Jesus did not do any miracles, then what *did* he do?

To consider:

Jesus feeds the hungry.
In what ways do I do this?
Can I do more?

Day 16

Mark 6.45-56: The walking on the water

There are a lot of similarities between this story and the calming of the storm:

- Both are miracles performed by Jesus on the Sea of Galilee.
- Both accounts have hidden meanings. These work like a code: they are full of references to the Old Testament which would have been picked up by Mark's first readers.
- Both stories are Christological: they are about who Jesus is.

Let's consider the hidden meanings of this story first.

Old Testament ideas behind the walking on the water

The key words of *water* and *fear* feature in this account and in the calming of the storm. In the Jewish Bible, God was said to have power over water, and people's reaction to God's activity was characterised as fear. We explored these on Day 10.

Psalm 77.19 says:

> You [God] walked through the waves;
> You crossed the deep sea.

This is exactly what Jesus does here.

When Jesus approaches the disciples, he intends to '*pass by*' them. This is more than just a detail; the words contain loud echoes of the Old Testament:

- God makes his 'glory' or presence *pass by* Moses (Exodus 33.19-23);
- God *passes by* the mountain top where Elijah was camped (1 Kings 19.11-22);
- Job says, 'God passes by, but I cannot see him' (Job 9.11).
- Jesus calls to the disciples, 'It is I! Do not be afraid' (6.50). The Greek words Mark uses for 'It is I' are simply 'I AM' in the Greek. This is what God calls himself in Exodus 3.14. (And in the Septuagint, the Greek translation of the Old Testament which Mark knew, the Greek words are identical.)

If you add all this together, Mark is showing that what Jesus does is what God does. It is a short step from this to concluding that Jesus and God are the same person.

Persecution

There are a lot of references in Mark to Christians being persecuted. So this story works on a number of levels. It's not just a miracle story; it also acts as a parable for Christians facing victimisation and death. Mark's fellow Christians may well have felt like the disciples, struggling against the waves which seemed to threaten their lives. But Mark is saying Jesus will strengthen them, just as he saved the disciples here.

To consider:

Jesus says, 'It is I! Do not be afraid'
At the end of Matthew's Gospel, the risen Jesus promises his followers, 'I am always with you, to the end of time.'

Day 17

Mark 7.1-23: What makes a person unclean?

This is Mark's second long collection of Jesus' teaching; the first was the parables of the Kingdom in 4.1-34. For the time being, it rounds off the theme of the authorities' hostility to Jesus.

A central concept in Judaism is that God has said some things are *unclean*, while other things are *clean*. Unclean things barred you from public worship for a period. People steered clear of anything that might make them unclean, in order to please God. Clean things were safe to use. This idea went back to the Torah, which laid down rules about which things were which.

There were unclean foods, such as pork; unclean diseases, such as leprosy; and unclean actions, such as touching a dead body. A good Jew saw the laws as expressions of God's will: the way he intended his people to live, and to mark them off from the Gentiles.

By the time of Jesus, a lot of traditional laws had grown up alongside the Torah, which were supposed to help people to keep it. Mark calls these 'the tradition of the elders' (7.3). The Pharisees thought that these traditions were almost as important as the Torah itself.

Mark's account shows his readers where Jesus stood in this argument. As we have come to expect by now, his attitude towards the whole business is a very radical one. Like the story of the Sabbath corn (2.23-28), it begins with the disciples annoying the Pharisees.

The Pharisees are angry because Jesus' disciples have not been washing their hands in the traditional way before eating. In fact, only priests had to wash their hands like this. The Pharisees are behaving as though they were priests, as an extra expression of their devotion to God. And they expected Jesus' disciples to do as they did. (Mark explains Jewish customs, which shows his readers are Gentiles. Jews would not need the explanation.)

Because of the way Mark has arranged the story, Jesus' answer does not come straight away. But when it does (verse 15), it is a bombshell:

> Nothing that goes into someone from outside can make the person unclean; it is the things that come out of someone that make that person unclean.

As usual, the disciples do not at first understand what Jesus is saying. Mark says that Jesus explained things for them.

True religion is not a matter of rules and regulations. God is not really bothered about how people wash their hands. For Jesus, the things that really matter are the things which come from someone's heart. What matters is not dirty hands, but the sins people have within them. The Pharisees have got it all wrong. God's interest goes deeper.

In the rest of the story, Mark has been trying to show how dangerous it is to forget this. In theory, the Pharisees understood that loving God and loving your neighbour were more important than rules about washing hands. The trouble was that they concentrated so hard on keeping every last rule that they couldn't see the wood for the trees.

In verses 6-13, Mark gives his readers an example. The traditions of the Pharisees said that if you made a solemn oath that something belonged to God – it was 'Corban' (or 'Korban') – it could not be used for anything else, even to help somebody. So although God's commandments said that people were to honour their parents, if someone had money they needed, but did not want to give it to them, he had only to say it was Corban – and they couldn't get at it! It was a perfect example of how religious rules could be used to get people off doing what God really wanted.

Jesus says that people who behave like this is hypocrites: those who say one thing and do another. They 'put aside the commandment of God to observe human traditions'. They are like the people in the time of Isaiah, who honoured God with their words, but were far away from his in their hearts.

Jesus may be thinking of an actual case when he talks about Corban. The rabbis later banned this kind of misuse of oaths. Jesus' criticism of the Pharisees is perfectly in keeping with Jewish practice.

Jesus, Christians and the Torah

Jesus does not seem to have much time for the traditional teachings which the Pharisees thought were so important. However, in the story of the healing of the leper (1.40-45), Jesus follows the Torah. He does so on other occasions too, like going to the synagogue on the Sabbath.

Jesus and his first disciples were all Jews. Most later Christians were Gentiles. One of the biggest issues in the early Church was to decide whether these Gentle Christians should keep all the religious laws of the Torah. Some Jewish Christians thought they should; others disagreed. This is one of the key themes in the letters of St Paul, and in the Acts of the Apostles.

Mark says Jesus 'pronounced all foods clean'. The problem is: if Jesus had made it so obvious that he was overruling the Torah's laws and saying they no longer applied, why did the early Christians debate it for so long? They would have had their answer.

It looks likely that this is Mark's interpretation. He may be right. But lots of Jewish Christians clearly *didn't* think Jesus had abolished the food laws; they felt that they should be imposed on Gentile Christians.

In the end, Mark's view won. It would have been impractical to insist on Gentile converts keeping the Torah. Many in the Gentile world realised that their polytheism – worship of many gods – was nonsense. Their philosophers had demonstrated that there could be only one God. And these Gentiles wanted a monotheistic religion with high moral standards. Many were attracted to Judaism, but Judaism was not really a missionary faith: it did not seek to make converts. And the Torah worried these Gentiles: unsurprisingly, men were alarmed at the thought of having to be circumcised (and there were no anaesthetics). They were puzzled by the food laws, too. So, when the Christians decided not to keep the food laws, and to replace circumcision with baptism, Gentiles came to them in huge numbers.

Jesus comes across as being very stern here. Is he being anti-Jewish?

Not really. Judaism is full of Jewish teachers who criticised religious practices of their time. The Old Testament prophets are outraged by people who offer all the right prayers and sacrifices but ignore human need. Their criticisms are far stronger than Jesus'. So Jesus is actually picking up a theme that runs through the whole of the Old Testament: loving your neighbour is more important than being a religious busybody. (For an example, have a look at Amos 5. 10-24.)

To consider:

'It is what comes out of someone that makes that person unclean. For it is from within, from the heart, that evil intentions emerge: fornication, theft, murder, adultery, avarice, malice, deceit, indecency, envy, slander, pride, folly. All these evil things come from within and make a person unclean.'

Day 18

Mark 7.24-37: Jesus and the Gentiles

The Syro-Phoenician woman (7.24-30)

It seems that news about Jesus had travelled as far as the Gentile town of Tyre. Even in this Gentile area people had heard of him. One of them, a woman, comes to see him.

Jews in Jesus' time thought women were second-class citizens. A *Gentile* woman, who did not even worship the same God, was even worse! But Jesus did not think like this. For him, people are people. It does not matter what sex or race they are.

The woman asks Jesus for an exorcism. Jesus' reply looks very strange at first:

> Let the children first be fed, for it is not right to take the children's bread and throw it to the dogs.

In other words, 'Let's give the Jews what they need first of all. It's not fair to give what the Jews need to dogs like you Gentiles.'

The woman replies, 'Even the dogs under the table eat the children's leftovers!' In other words, 'Even if we *are* dogs, at least dogs get something!'

There's no sense in which Jesus is being racist; he's being ironic. The woman picks up on the joke, and adds a punchline. (In any case, the word Mark uses means a pet dog, not a wild dog.)

The early Christians believed that Gentiles were included in God's family, the Kingdom of God. But St Paul's letter to the Romans shows that the Good News should be preached 'to the Jews first, and then to the Gentiles' (Romans 1.16). Mark shares this view. (It's interesting that, if Mark the evangelist was John Mark, he knew Paul well. It would not then be surprising that he has the same outlook as Paul.)

The deaf mute (7.31-37)

There are stories about other healers in the ancient world using saliva or touch to cure people. Matthew and Luke, who both used Mark as a major source, omit this account, perhaps because it makes Jesus look too like other alleged 'healers' of his day.

This story would have reminded Mark's readers of a passage in the prophet Isaiah, which was thought to predict what would happen when the Messiah came:

> The blind will be able to see, and the deaf will hear.   (Isaiah 35.5)

And, once again, Mark gives Jesus' words in Aramaic (*ephphatha*). The early Christians switched their language quickly to Greek as soon as the gospel was preached to the Gentiles. The Aramaic words probably indicate the story was in circulation very early: in Israel, before the Gentile mission took off. This is good evidence for the story's being historical.

Notes

In the Greek of 7.27, Jesus talks about the children's *bread*. We saw when we examined the feeding of the 5000 that *bread* would have suggested the Last Supper to Mark's readers. That bread – the bread of Jesus' body – will be given to both Jews and Gentiles in the Church.

There is actually a problem with saying that Jesus meant 'pet dog', even though Mark uses the word. In Aramaic, the language Jesus spoke, there is only one word for 'dog', and that could be used as an insult (pariah, not doggy!). The flaw in this argument is that the woman was not a Jew, so it is unlikely Jesus spoke to her in Aramaic. Jesus presumably spoke to her in Greek. Recent research shows that Jesus grew up near a town called Sepphoris, which had a large number of traders who spoke Greek. As a carpenter, Jesus would have conducted business there, and so must have known enough of the language to be able to do so.

Mark is again thinking of the Messianic secret in 7.36 but it looks very odd here. For one thing, people do not do what Jesus says: instead, they spread the news around. If Jesus normally told people to keep quiet because he did not want them to get the wrong idea about his Messiahship, why does he tell a Gentile crowd to be quiet? They were not expecting a Messiah. The answer may be that although Gentiles were not waiting for a Messiah, they got very excited about people who were thought to be wonder workers, and Jesus did not want this label either.

To consider:

'There is neither Jew nor Greek,
slave nor free,
male nor female,
for you are all one in Christ Jesus.' (Galatians 3.28)

Day 19

The feeding of the 4000 (8.1-10)

It is almost certain that this is a variant account of the feeding of the 5000; the wording is just too similar for it to be a different event.

The question is, why tell the story twice?

Once again, the solution seems to be in the symbolism. The 'bread' Jesus produces for the crowds reminds the readers of the bread of his body, given to his followers at the Last Supper and at the Eucharist. The feeding of the 5000 takes place on the shores of the Sea of Galilee, which means the crowd was Jewish. Here, the miracle takes place near the Decapolis (Ten Towns), a Gentile area. The bread of life, then, is for both Jews and Gentiles in the Kingdom of God.

The Pharisees ask for a sign (8.11-13)

As usual, the Pharisees are presented as being deeply suspicious. If Jesus is sent from God, he should confirm it by some sort of sign from God. But Jesus has been performing signs all the time; the evidence is there for anyone who wants to see. He is not going to perform miracles to order – and even if he did, the Pharisees still wouldn't believe it.

In the story of Jesus' rejection at Nazareth, Jesus was unable to perform any miracles in his home town because of the people's lack of faith. The Pharisees have no faith either. All they want to do is to catch him out. They don't accept the Kingdom of God gladly: they're hanging back. In Mark 4.11-12, Jesus said the disciples had the secret of the Kingdom of God, but there was another group: 'those outside', who did not understand the parables, who could look and look and see nothing, listen and listen and hear nothing. Not only do this group not understand the parables; they do not understand the miracles either.

Miracles on their own prove nothing. Mark is saying you have to have faith to understand them. When Jesus was performing exorcisms, the religious leaders thought he was possessed by the Devil (3.22). If people are determined to think badly of someone, they can usually find some excuse. Even if Jesus gave the Pharisees the sign they asked for, he could not win against their closed minds.

The yeast of the Pharisees and of Herod (8.14-21)

This passage is not easy. The meaning seems to be something like this:

The rabbis sometimes used the word 'yeast' to mean 'bad ideas' or 'evil intentions'. Jesus is therefore warning the disciples to beware of the Pharisees' way of thinking. The 'yeast... of Herod' is less clear. It may refer not to Herod Antipas himself, but to his followers, the Herodians. Unfortunately, we now know nothing whatsoever about them and what Jesus meant is now lost to us.

The disciples have no idea what Jesus is talking about. 'Is he cross because we forgot the sandwiches?' someone suggests, perhaps flippantly. Jesus is not impressed; they really ought to know better by now. After all, they have seen the feeding miracles, when there was enough food for everybody. They should learn to trust him.

He then asks the disciples about the number of baskets of leftovers from when he fed the crowds. Twelve were left by the 5000; seven were left by the 4000. Twelve was a significant number for Jews: there were twelve tribes of Israel, which again underlines that the 5000 were Jews. 'Seven' is less easy, though there were said to be seventy nations of the Gentiles, so it could be said to be a 'Gentile number' and emphasise that the 4000 were non-Jews. (This may have been more convincing for first century readers, when there was a greater interest in number symbolism than there is today.) The Kingdom of God is for everyone, Jews and Gentiles alike. Perhaps the particular 'yeast' or wrong idea of the Pharisees is that God is only interested in the Jewish people.

But this is a difficult passage and it's not possible to be certain what it means.

The blind man at Bethsaida (8.22-26)

This story is only found in Mark; Matthew and Luke cut it. Perhaps they felt it was not spectacular enough; the cure comes gradually, not immediately. They also leave out the cure of the deaf mute (7.31-37), where Jesus also uses spittle to effect a cure. This was a feature of pagan miracle stories, another possible reason for Matthew and Luke's censoring it. Mark may have thought of the miracles as a pair. They would have reminded his readers about some words of Isaiah, which were linked to the coming of the Kingdom:

> The blind will be able to see

Once again, Mark ends with an instruction related to the Messianic secret: the man is not even to return to the village.

The account has a symbolic meaning too. Mark is about to begin a long section of the Gospel in which the disciples come to appreciate more fully who Jesus really is. Their eyes, too, will be gradually opened.

To consider:

'Beware of the yeast of the Pharisees.' The Pharisees are presented as being convinced that they are right, self-righteous, and willing to condemn. Those are the attitudes we are warned against.

Day 20

Mark 8.27-9.1: Who do you say I am?

Peter's reply to this question is a turning-point in Mark's Gospel:

You are the Christ.

This is at last the right answer – not just to Jesus' question, but to all the other times when people have asked, 'Who is this?' And yet Jesus orders his disciples to tell no one about him. Who Jesus is remains a secret, although the disciples have begun to share it.

But Peter and the other disciples mess it up again. Their ideas about the Christ are way off, but they can't get them out of their heads. The Messiah will not wage war on Rome, or wipe out all evildoers. For the first time, Jesus teaches them that he will suffer, die and rise again.

Even though Peter has just called Jesus 'the Christ' or 'the Messiah' (the words mean the same thing), Jesus calls himself 'the Son of Man', the title he prefers. And the Son of Man will suffer and die. But why? Mark gives his readers absolutely no explanation here. However, Jesus says that it must happen. It is part of God's plan, even if it seems a mystery at first. That Jesus will also rise from the dead is a completely new teaching. As far as we know, nobody at the time of Jesus expected the Messiah to die for others, let alone to rise again.

When Peter called Jesus the Christ, he certainly did not mean the sort of Christ Jesus himself had in mind. Like everybody else, he seems to have thought of a military Son of David. He had seen a great future for his friend. Now it seems that all his hopes are to be dashed. He tries to tell Jesus off, to make him change his mind, but Jesus rounds on him angrily and calls him *Satan*.

If people want to be true disciples, they must be prepared to follow him to the death. If Jesus is prepared to sacrifice everything for others, his disciples must be prepared to do so too. If you gain the whole world but lose your soul, it is a very poor exchange. The Greek word Mark uses for soul is *psyche*, which means *self* or *life*, as well as *soul*. Jesus is saying that his disciples must be willing to 'give themselves up', to go with him whatever the cost. Becoming 'selfless' is a painful business, like carrying a cross. This image – taking up your cross – comes from the ritual surrounding Roman crucifixions. The condemned criminal, carrying the crossbeam, was a common sight. So it means 'being willing to go to your death'. Commitment to Jesus must be total.

To refuse to follow Jesus is a serious matter. It was like losing your true self. What was really going to count in the end was whether someone accepted Jesus, or refused him. The Son of Man will come, and everyone will be judged.

Mark 9.1

This probably wins the prize for being the most difficult verse in the whole Gospel. It reads:

> And he said to them, 'I tell you the truth, some who are standing here will not taste death before they see the Kingdom of God come with power.'

Not easy, and it has caused endless debate among New Testament scholars. The problem is that when Jesus taught about the Kingdom of God, he sometimes implied that it had begun with his own work. At other times, he talks about it as though it is totally in the future. It would not arrive finally until the Son of Man came in glory at the end of the world.

The most obvious meaning of 9.1 is that Jesus expected the end of the world, and the final coming of God's Kingdom, before some of his audience were dead. Obviously, this did not happen. Reading the New Testament makes it pretty clear that lots of early Christians expected the second coming, the parousia, very soon. They then had to come to terms with the idea that it was not going to happen as quickly as they thought.

So does this mean Jesus got it wrong?

Perhaps. Christianity says that Jesus is fully human and fully God. Some theologians say that must mean he could make mistakes, which is part of being human.

Or perhaps this verse does not contain the genuine words of Jesus. Instead, they reflect the early Christian idea that the parousia was just round the corner.

Or they *are* genuine words of Jesus, but he's actually talking about the Transfiguration, which happens next. Or perhaps he means the resurrection.

Or (again!) the Greek can be translated to mean that Jesus' listeners will realise that the Kingdom has *already* come.

It is not certain which of these ideas is correct, and we can only speculate.

To consider:

'Who do you say that I am?'

Day 21

Mark 9.2-13: The Transfiguration

The Greek text of Mark says that Jesus 'underwent a metamorphosis'. The account clearly shows the Jesus is the Son of God, but also that the Son of God must suffer.

The passage works as an elaborate code. People who knew the Old Testament, like Mark's first readers, would have spotted the hidden meanings at once, though they're a little less obvious to us today. Let's examine what the story is trying to say.

Jesus is the Son of God

1. Jesus took his disciples up a *mountain*. This has been identified as either Mount Tabor or Mount Hermon is Israel, but it also has a symbolic meaning. In the Old Testament, many of the manifestations of God, the theophanies, occured on mountains; indeed, it was there that Elijah and Moses both had experiences of God (Exodus 24, 1 Kings 19.8-9). So, the account is a theophany or something very similar.

2. When Jesus' appearance changed, the disciples realised that he was the same person, but had a deeper insight into his true nature. His clothes became dazzling white; white was the (symbolic) colour ascribed to heavenly things. Angels were said to dress in white (cf Matthew 28.2-3). Moreover, Paul says in his letter to the Philippians that Jesus had a 'body of glory' after the resurrection (Philippians 3.21); it may be that this is what Mark is thinking of here. The account makes it quite clear that the human Jesus is also the Son of God.

3. The disciples, perhaps understandably, are terrified. Once again, though, this underlines that the transfiguration is something like a theophany; the Israelites' reaction to the manifestations of God was one of fear (Exodus 20.1-21).

4. Peter's wanting to build three tents seems bizarre at first, but again, there's a symbolism at work. The word for 'tent' can also be translated at 'tabernacle'. The Jewish festival of Tabernacles remembers the Exodus, when the Jews camped out in tents – and, as they were being looked after by God, 'tents' came to symbolise the presence of God among his people. During the Exodus, there was even a tent shrine for God: the Tabernacle. The prophet Ezekiel predicted a time when God 'would live with his people',

and the Hebrew word he uses means 'to live in a tent' (Ezekiel 37.27). So Peter recognises that something like this is happening now. (Incidentally, in his description of the incarnation, John says 'the Word became flesh, and dwelt among us' (John 1.14). The words John uses for 'dwelt among us' literally translate as 'pitched his tent among us'.)

5. In the Old Testament, God's glory meant his beauty and power; God was so great that no one could look at him and survive. As a result, he was sometimes said to veil his presence by a *cloud* (called the *shekinah*) to shield the people from harm. Mark's mention of the cloud isn't just saying something about the weather; it symbolises the presence of God (cf Exodus 33.20, 24.15-18.)

6. The heavenly voice at Jesus' baptism had said that Jesus was the Son of God (1.11). This is the only other time that Mark says that God speaks from heaven. Here, God the Father tells the disciples who Jesus is, and that they must 'listen to him'. And what Jesus has just been teaching them is that the Son of God must suffer (8.31-38).

The Son of God must suffer

1. Elijah and Moses appear and talk with Jesus. The early Christians believed that both were connected with the Messiah, and here they are. Moses had said God would send a new prophet whom people should 'listen to' (Deuteronomy 18.13); the fact that the voice from heaven says the disciples should 'listen to' Jesus may also show that Mark believed Jesus to be the 'prophet' predicted by Moses. People thought Elijah would return to herald the coming of the Messiah (Malachi 4.5-6).

2. Elijah and Moses both suffered for their faith; the Son of God also has to suffer. But by Jesus' time, the belief had grown up that both Elijah and Moses survived death. (2 Kings 2.1-17 says this fairly explicitly about Elijah; Moses' death is recorded in Deuteronomy 34.5-6, but it goes on to say 'no man knows the place of his burial to this day'. This was later taken to mean that he had not been buried at all, but had been carried into heaven.)

3. Jesus tells his disciples not to tell anyone what they had seen 'until the Son of Man has risen from death'. The Son of God is a figure of glory and power, but he is also the Son of Man, whose mission is to suffer and die. Only after that has happened will people understand what his work really means.

4. The disciples have just seen that Jesus is the Son of God. And

they have seen Elijah. But where was Elijah before Jesus came?

Jesus replied, 'Elijah has already come.' Mark's readers would know he meant John the Baptist.

What sort of a story is the transfiguration?

Opinions vary. It will probably not surprise you that liberal Biblical scholars regard the account as unhistorical. The technical term they give to this kind of story is a 'myth', which isn't quite the same as saying it's 'not true'. A myth is a story which conveys religious truths, even if it didn't happen. According to this view, the transfiguration is an attempt to express beliefs in Jesus in the form of a story. Perhaps a better word would be 'parable', although this is a parable about Jesus, rather than one told by him.

If the transfiguration is not a myth, it's not clear whether it's to be taken as a subjective or an objective experience: whether it was something concrete that happened on a Galilean mountain, or whether it was a genuine experience, but one that took place within the minds of the disciples. It's interesting that Matthew calls the transfiguration a 'vision', which suggests he saw it as more of a subjective reality.

It's been suggested that this was originally an account of one of the appearances of the risen Jesus. This isn't likely; the resurrection appearances are actually rather more subdued than the transfiguration.

To consider:

'And the Word became flesh and dwelt among us, full of grace and truth; we have beheld his glory, glory as of the only Son from the Father' (John 1.14).

Day 22

Mark 9.14-29: The faithless people

The theme of this miracle story is the need for faith. This is shown in three ways:

1. The people need faith. When it comes to the boy's healing, they do not trust God. Once again, Mark emphasises Jesus' human emotions: his reaction to the situation certainly seems to be one of anger, or perhaps exasperation. In verse 19, he talks as though he were God passing judgement on his people; the Old Testament frequently shows God upbraiding Israel through the prophets for not trusting in him: cf Jeremiah 5.23. One rabbi said that the Messiah's generation would be particularly faithless. And Mark believes it is because of this lack of faith that they fail to realise who Jesus is, and have him killed.
2. The disciples need faith. Jesus gave the disciples the authority to heal (3.15). But perhaps they needed to pray more, to rely more on God's power, before the healings would work. This verse may be intended to give instructions for early Christian healers; Mark is saying you could only cast out violent demons if you pray. Some manuscripts add to the instructions, and say the disciples need 'prayer *and fasting*'. These words are usually omitted by English translations – and rightly, as they're not by Mark.
3. The boy's father asks for more faith. He does believe, but asks for Jesus' help because his faith is inadequate. Mark's first readers were probably being persecuted; like the boy's father, they need to trust God, especially when everything looks bleak.

Mark places this miracle story right after his account of the Transfiguration. With Peter, James and John, Jesus returns to ordinary people and their problems. The whole section is rather like Exodus 32-33.6: Moses was speaking to God on a mountain and, like Jesus, he came down to find God's people behaving as though they had no faith at all. Moses found they had made idols to worship; Jesus finds they have no faith in God's power to heal.

When Jesus arrives, the people 'were greatly surprised'. Mark may think this is just because he arrives suddenly. However, it may again be an echo of the Exodus story, as the Torah says Moses' face shone after he had been speaking with God. Perhaps Mark thought Jesus was still radiant after the Transfiguration.

First Century readers would have agreed with Mark's view that the boy was possessed by a demon. A modern diagnosis might be different: we would probably say the boy was an epileptic. It's not difficult to imagine that people in Jesus' day would have thought epilepsy was caused by the attacks of a particularly vicious demon. But Jesus heals the boy. Curing epilepsy is quite extraordinary; even today, there is treatment, but no cure. Mark believes Jesus is able to heal people because of who he is.

To consider:

Lord, I have faith. Help me where faith falls short.

Day 23

Mark 9.30-50: Some teachings of Jesus.

Mark now gives his readers some short examples of Jesus' sayings. They seem to be very loosely connected, so it seems likely that they originally came from different occasions in Jesus' ministry. Mark has collected them and strung them together like beads on a necklace – perhaps because he did not know when they first happened. Sometimes he has put sayings together because they have the same theme or key word, like 'salt' or 'fire'.

The second passion prediction (9.30-32)

This is slightly different from the first passion prediction in 8.31-33. Here, Jesus adds that he will be 'delivered into the hands of men'. Someone is going to do that. There is a traitor in their midst.

Who is the greatest? (9.33-37)

Capernaum was Jesus' home base for most of the ministry. In the account, the disciples are ashamed of themselves: they are beginning to realise that Jesus' Kingdom is not about power, even if they do not always live up to the ideal. Jesus knows that the lesson needs to be repeated if it is to be learned properly. Patiently, he sits down (a rabbi would sometimes do this when he was teaching something important) and calls the twelve to him.

Jesus says that true greatness means being a servant of all.

The Kingdom turns all the usual values upside down. If someone is ambitious, he or she should look for the lowest place and the best opportunity to serve others. In Mark's story, Jesus makes this clear by taking the child in his arms. The point is that children need to be looked after: they are not powerful, or rich, or influential. But by welcoming them, the disciples welcome him. The child stands for all those, including children, who need help and are too easily overlooked.

'Whoever is not against us is for us' (9.38-41)

The early Church had a problem with non-Christians who claimed to drive out devils using Jesus' name. The idea was that his name was itself so powerful that demons were exorcised when they heard it.

Things were more difficult when the exorcisms looked like black magic (Acts 19.11-20), so the early Christians needed Jesus' advice to solve the problem.

The next saying, which may originally have been given on another occasion, speaks of acts of kindness by non-Christians:

> For truly I tell you, whoever gives you a cup of water to drink because you bear the name of Christ will by no means lose the reward. (9.41)

There is actually quite a lot in this verse. For a start, it is one of the very few occasions in Mark when Jesus actually calls himself the 'Christ'. It is not true to say that he rejected the title: he accepted it, as long as people understood what it really meant.

Far from having a go at people who are outside their group, but who are really on their side, the disciples should be grateful for even a cup of water, given because they belong to Jesus.

Many Christians lay great stress on those passages in the New Testament which seem to say that only Christians will go to heaven (see Romans 1.16-17). However, there are other passages, including this saying of Jesus, that imply this is not the case. You do not have to be a Christian to receive 'the reward' of heaven. This is shown clearly in the parable of the sheep and the goats in Matthew's Gospel (Matthew 25.31-46): those who have been kind and generous to others are admitted to heaven. Even the smallest act of kindness, like giving a drink of water to someone who's thirsty, will be rewarded. There is no mention of the reward's being limited only to Christians.

The Roman Catholic Church teaches that non-Christians can and do go to heaven. Many other Christians are uncomfortable with the idea.

Temptations to sin (9.42-48)

Jesus gives some frightening warnings here. Some things people do mean they will go to hell.

Our English word 'hell' translates the word 'Gehenna', which was a valley to the east of Jerusalem. In ancient Israel, children were burnt alive there as sacrifices to the god Molech (2 Kings 23.10). This had stopped long before Jesus' time, and the place had become a dump where rubbish was burnt. Because of this, Gehenna was a place of fire, and the word was used to describe the place where evil people would be punished after death.

The idea in these verses is this. If you cause someone – including yourself – to sin, you are in danger of being punished.

First, Jesus warns his followers not to make other people sin. It is terrible to be drowned with a millstone round your neck, but it is even more terrible to cause 'one of these little ones' to sin. Mark has placed these sayings close to the account of Jesus' taking a child in his arms, so 'little ones' may well mean children (it seems to do so in the context in which it has been placed). However, as Jesus called his followers 'little ones' or 'children', it may mean any Christian. A millstone was a huge piece of rock turned by a donkey to grind corn. People were sometimes executed in the Roman Empire in the way Jesus describes.

Jesus then warns his followers not to let themselves sin. They want to enter 'life': eternal life in the Kingdom of God. If Mark's first readers were being persecuted for their faith, it would have been very easy to sin by falling away from Christianity. Here, they are warned not to.

First century Jews considered that different parts of the body tempted people to different sins. For example, the eye tempted people to lust (Proverbs 6.16-19). Jesus is not literally telling his followers to maim themselves. What he means is that the life of the Kingdom is the most important thing there is. It is worth far more than a hand, or a foot, or an eye.

It's interesting that this is the only passage in Mark where Jesus talks directly about hell. The later Gospels, especially Matthew, include a lot more material. Perhaps Mark did not think the subject was as important as some other Christians did.

(Verses 44 and 46 are identical to verse 48. They are left out by some Greek manuscripts of Mark and were probably added later.)

Salt (9.49-50)

These seem to be separate sayings of Jesus, which Mark has collected together because they have the same key word: salt. They are very hard to understand and we can only guess at what they originally meant.

Because everyone will be salted with fire. (9.49)

Sacrifices to God were held in the Jerusalem Temple. They were made pure (acceptable to God) by adding *salt* (Leviticus 2.13). If you heat metal in a *fire*, the pure metal will separate from everything else. The verse might mean that Christians should be pure. Perhaps 'fire' is an image of persecution, as though Christians who suffer the fire of persecution will be pure. But it's very difficult to be sure.

> Salt is good; but if the salt has lost its saltiness, how can you make it salty again? (9.50a)

There was another reason why people in Jesus' time thought salt was pure. It came from the purest things: the sea and the sun (which evaporates the sea water and leaves the salt behind). The saying may mean that Jesus' followers must not become impure, or they will fail in their job to make the world pure. And if they become impure, how can they become pure again?

(Strictly speaking, salt cannot lose it saltiness. But this is not a problem for the saying. The salt from the Dead Sea is not pure; there are lots of other things in it. So it is possible to have something that looks like salt when the real salt has dissolved.)

> Have salt in yourselves, and be at peace with one another. (9.50b)

'Be at peace with one another' is straightforward. It is practically impossible to know what 'have salt in yourselves' means. The options are:
- the salt of purity
- the salt of kindness
- the salt of being willing to be persecuted.

We just don't know. The Good News Bible suggests the salt of friendship, but this is very unlikely.

The 'salt' sayings raise a question. When Mark recorded them, did he know what they meant? Perhaps – but then again, perhaps not. It could be that he has included them for no other reason than that they are sayings of Jesus, even if their meaning was lost. If so, it suggests that the evangelists were a great deal more accurate than the liberal scholars would hold. They wanted to record the words of Jesus even when they no longer comprehended them.

To consider:

'If anyone would be first, he must be the last and the servant of all.'

Day 24

Mark 10.1-16: Marriage and children

Mark says the Pharisees were on the warpath again. This time, they try to drag Jesus into an argument about divorce, perhaps trying to get him into trouble with Herod Antipas, who had divorced and remarried. They also want to tangle Jesus up in an argument on the subject between the rabbis, and hoped they would trip him up over some legal point.

The rabbis disagreed violently over divorce. The book of Deuteronomy in the Torah said a man could divorce his wife is she was 'guilty of some shameful conduct' (Deuteronomy 24.1). (Jewish law does not allow a woman to divorce her husband.) The question was, how bad did this 'shameful conduct' have to be?

One side followed the strict teachings of a rabbi called Shammai, who said that the 'shameful conduct' meant adultery and nothing else. The other side followed Rabbi Hillel. They said the 'shameful conduct' meant almost anything the husband did not like: talking to a man she did not know or even spoiling a meal. Not surprisingly, Hillel's ideas were more popular than Shammai's. (Human beings usually prefer easy options and there's nothing nicer than behaving badly and kidding yourself that you're in the right.) As a result, women were frequently very badly treated: they were divorced for very minor reasons, they were insecure within marriage, and divorce brought terrible disgrace.

Jesus side-steps the trap the Pharisees have laid for him. Instead of arguing with them about the rules in Deuteronomy, he takes them right back to the beginning, when God created men and women. He refers them back to the book of Genesis (specifically, to verses 1.27 and 2.24). The Torah's laws on divorce came about only because things had gone wrong; marriage itself is built into the framework of the universe. It is how God has created the world. For this reason, divorce should not happen at all.

Divorce and Christians today

It's clear from this passage that Jesus wanted the women of his day to live in love, security and respect. They should not be divorced for trivial reasons.

There is a problem, though, for today's Christians. Did Jesus mean to ban divorce in the first century, when things had got ridiculously out of hand? Or did he mean to ban divorce for everyone, for all time?

Even in the early Church, it seems, this had become an issue. Matthew's version of Jesus' teaching is different. There, he says:

> Whoever divorces his wife, except for unchastity, and marries another, commits adultery... Not everyone can accept this teaching, but only those to whom it is given.
> (Matthew 19.9, 11)

Divorce *is* allowed by Jesus, according to Matthew, if there is 'unchastity'. It's not clear what this means. The Greek word is *porneia*, meaning 'sexual immorality', which is fairly vague. And not everyone can 'accept' this teaching. Does this mean it doesn't apply to everybody, or that some just refuse to accept it?

Most New Testament scholars take the view that the original teaching is given in Mark: historically, Jesus banned divorce totally. Matthew has softened the teaching, allowing divorce in certain (rather unclear) circumstances. Matthew was writing later than Mark. By then, some Christians may have found Jesus' teaching too difficult to keep, so the later Gospel has softened Jesus' ban. (Matthew probably would have seen this as explaining what he thought Jesus really meant. He isn't trying to mislead people.)

Mark, too, seems to have tried to clarify Jesus' teaching. He appears to have added verse 12 because Roman law, unlike Jewish law, did allow women to divorce their husbands.

Christians have always had a hard time trying to square the experience of ordinary men and women with the teachings of Jesus.

The Roman Catholic Church follows what Jesus said in Mark. As we have seen, this is most likely to be what Jesus actually taught. Divorce and remarriage are not allowed for Catholics. However, the Catholic Church does allow for the possibility that there may never have been a real marriage in the first place, even though the couple went through a wedding ceremony. For example, the husband or wife might not have understood the marriage vows, or might have been forced into making them, or the marriage was never consummated. In circumstances like these, the Church can declare an *annulment*. This is a solemn declaration that, from the beginning, no real marriage existed.

Catholics whose marriages have been annulled are free to marry in church, even if the person to whom they were previously 'married' is still alive.

Divorce and remarriage is allowed by other Churches. The Church of England and the rest of the Anglican Communion, the Orthodox and most Protestant Churches allow it. They all take a dim view, though, of marriages being broken up by the selfish or unkind behaviour or one or both of the partners.

All Christians, however, stress that marriage is a serious undertaking, and couples whose marriages are in trouble need to be cared for and helped as much as possible.

Children and the Kingdom (10.13-16)

Mark does not tell us why the disciples tried to stop people bringing their children to Jesus; perhaps they thought it was wasting his time. But Jesus was cross with them (notice again how Mark emphasises his human reactions). He welcomes the children, and blesses them:

Let the children come to me, and do not stop them, because the Kingdom of God belongs to such as these. (10.14)

Why 'to such as these'? One answer is the Jesus thought his disciples should learn from some of the qualities children have. Young children (the word Mark uses means someone under twelve) are generally eager to learn, trusting, and loving towards their parents. These are the attitudes the disciples should have towards God.

But this does not seem to be enough. It is easy to be sentimental about children − but most of us know how difficult the nicest child can be on a bad day. Jesus welcomed children because they were needy and powerless. Children had no standing in the Jewish society or his day, or in the eyes of the religious authorities. The disciples behave in the way we would expect men of their time to behave. Because of this, Jesus makes children the symbol of all the people the Kingdom is really for: the weak, the oppressed, the poor and the outcasts.

I assure you that whoever does not receive the Kingdom of God like a child will never enter it. (10.15)

Two explanations are suggested for this verse:
1. Children like to be given things. They very rarely turn their noses up at something done especially for them. This childlike openness is the proper attitude Jesus' listeners should have to God's gift of the Kingdom.
2. People should welcome the Kingdom of God as they would

welcome their own child, and as Jesus himself welcomes the children in this story.

It is difficult to tell which of these Mark meant. (Perhaps both.) Most people usually understand it in the first way described. In Matthew, Jesus says, 'Unless you change and become like children, you can never enter the Kingdom of Heaven' (Mathew 18.3)

To consider:

Am I quick to judge those whose marriages are in trouble?
Jesus welcomed children. Do I? Or do I find them irritating and a nuisance?

Day 25

Mark 10.17-31: Camels, needles and cash

If you were an alien who came to this planet, and watched a few hours' television, you would probably come to the conclusion that Earth people are obsessed with money: their rôle models are the ultra-rich; they think the more money they have, the better they are as people; and they follow a strange religion called Get and Spend.

There's nothing new in liking money. History seems to show that human beings have always wanted material possessions and can very easily get greedy. It isn't hard, either, for those who are less well off to become envious.

Jesus tells the rich man to give his money away. All of it. Jesus was pleased he kept the Torah, but he did not go far enough: money was the centre of his life.

Both the disciples and the rich man thought God wanted some people to be rich; wealth was a sign that God had blessed you. Yet the coming of the Kingdom of God changes things. If people want to join it, nothing must get in the way.   And being members of the Kingdom means they are responsible for others' welfare.

Peter says they've left everything to follow Jesus. (Mark doesn't tell us his tone of voice, but it certainly sounds like grumbling.) Those who want to be disciples may find lots of things get in the way: family, money, property – but people who give things up for Jesus' sake will be rewarded. There may be persecutions to go through, as Mark's Church may have experienced. Yet there will be many new 'brothers', 'sisters' and 'mothers' among the family of the Church community. And Jesus' followers will receive the ultimate reward: eternal life. Jesus concludes:

Many that are first will be last, and the last first.   (10.31)

The first – the rich and the powerful – are really the last. The last – the poor, the outcasts, the sinners – are really the first.

Those who will get into God's Kingdom first will not be those whom society thinks are the best. The first in will be those to whom society closes its doors, but for whom Christ's door is always open.

Notes

10.18. Christians believe Jesus is God. Why, then, does he say, 'No one is good but God alone'? Perhaps he did not like the man's flattery. If Jesus knew he was God, he did not tell everyone. However, when Mark says the rich man called Jesus 'good', he may be hinting at who Jesus really is.

10.24: The Revised Standard Version has 'how hard it is to enter the Kingdom of God' here. In other words, it's hard for *everybody*. Other translations follow some Greek manuscripts which say it's only hard 'for those who trust in riches'. Mark didn't write this later version, which changes the meaning.

10.25: It's sometimes suggested Jesus was talking about a gate in Jerusalem called 'The Needle's Eye', which was just wide enough to squeeze a camel through. He wasn't. There was no such gate. Jesus' vivid picture doesn't need explaining

Christianity and poverty today

In Luke's Gospel, Jesus says:

Blessed are you poor, for yours is the Kingdom of God.　　　(Luke 6.20)

The poor are our problem, and we must help. This is the view of all the major religions of the world.

There are various ways in which this can be done. It's not the place of a book like this to hector or to tell people what to do. Not all of us are in a position to help as much as others are. Christians all agree, though – or they're supposed to! – that the relief of poverty is a key obligation of their faith. What follows is a collection of suggestions of how this could be done, drawing on the views of a number of Christian writers. It's offered as something to reflect on. Here goes:

– Fairly obvious, this one: give to charity. Charities do welcome one off and occasional donations. However, they prefer standing orders and regular gifts because they're much more helpful in being able to budget. Gift aid helps, too.

– Find out more about poverty today; information can lead to change. Poverty is not something confined to poorer countries; it exists in Britain as well. Almost every charity today has a website, and they're worth browsing.

– Campaign. A major reason the poor stay poor is because it helps businesses. Not paying a fair wage saves money, keeps prices down, and makes more cash for companies. An even greater cause of poverty in the developing world is that developing countries pay huge sums of money in interest on loans to Western banks. Even if they have paid back the *amount* of the loan, the bank wants its interest. The money that goes to rich banks could be spent on housing, schools, and health care. (This situation could provide a modern meaning to what Jesus says in Mark 4.25: 'Whoever has will be given more; whoever does not have, even what he has will be taken from him.') Campaigning against such things is a key part of charities' work.

— Work for charities, either full time or part time.

— Buy fairly traded goods. Traidcraft, Oxfam and other organisations market Fairtrade goods: tea, coffee, chocolate, clothes, and lots of other products. They are *fairly* traded: the people who produce them in the developing world get a fair price for them. They are not kept poor by big businesses shopping around for the cheapest deal. Helping others, then, need not be a matter of charity; it can just mean buying things that you'd buy anyway. You just buy the fairly traded version. The major supermarkets increasingly stock fairly traded goods; from 2007, for example, every single banana sold by Sainsbury's was fairly traded.

— Vote in elections for the political party who'll do most to help the poor. It's easy to be cynical, but all the major political parties are serious about getting people out of poverty, both at home and abroad. (They can, however, disagree on the best way to do this and people can disagree as to which party does it most effectively.) Perhaps it is a Christian's duty to find out the details of exactly what a party intends to do about poverty, and then vote accordingly. It's easy to be simplistic or apathetic about politics but Christians are supposed to do what Jesus would want. The vast amounts of money at a government's disposal mean they can do more to help than charities can, who simply don't have the same resources. If governments can help the poor, Christians have a duty to take an interest in the political process – and that probably means we have a duty to vote, too. (A reason for a Christian to vote is not just because by doing so we can vote for what we judge to be the most Christian programme; it's also necessary to keep out the extremists, such as the neo-Nazi parties, whose policies can only be described as evil.)

How far should it go, though? Are Christians obliged to give everything away, like the rich man in Mark's account, and have just

97

the basic essentials?

It's certainly true that lots of Christians think this is what they *should* do, even if they don't manage it. Perhaps, today, the distinction made between essentials and inessentials needs to be considered carefully. For example, if you have a family, it would be irresponsible to say you should give away all or nearly all your income, if that meant your children went hungry, or they had to be cold in the winter because you'd given away the money for the gas bill. But most of us in the West have much more than we need.

If they're honest, most Christians would probably admit they don't do enough. They might set themselves a target, like giving away 10% of their income after tax. But even this wouldn't live up to what Jesus said. Christians are not allowed to rest on their laurels and be terribly pleased with themselves because they have a small monthly standing order to Christian Aid or CAFOD. There is always more that can be done.

It isn't clear from this passage whether Jesus expected everyone, like the rich man, to give away everything they have. However, in Luke's Gospel, Jesus meets someone else with too much money: a tax collector called Zacchaeus (Luke 19.1-10). Zacchaeus tells Jesus he will give away half of all his wealth to the poor, and if he's ripped anyone off, he'll pay them back four times as much. Jesus approves of this, and yet he doesn't tell Zacchaeus to give away the lot. So it does look as though Jesus expected people to be extremely generous, but not necessarily to give away everything.

(This is a guess, though, based on the evidence in the Gospels. It may not be right. It's always comfortable to try to tone down some of the more difficult demands of Jesus.)

To consider:

'Blessed are you poor, for yours is the Kingdom of God.'

Day 26

Mark 10.32-52: The road to Jerusalem

The stories in this section relate to Jesus' true purpose, which mystifies and unsettles the disciples.

The third passion prediction (10.32-34)

This, the third time Jesus speaks about his death, is the most detailed. The disciples and his other followers are confused and frightened. They still do not understand that the Messiah's purpose is to suffer and die for others. (Notice again, though, that Jesus calls himself 'the Son of Man' rather than 'the Messiah'.)

Jesus will be tortured and killed by the Roman (Gentile) rulers of Israel, but this will not be the end of him. Three days later, he will rise from death. Jesus strides on, walking ahead of his followers, knowing what awaits him.

(Jesus says he will rise to life 'three days' after he is put to death. We would say Friday to Sunday is two days later; Jews in the first century used an 'inclusive' method of counting, which would, as here, include the Friday as well.)

James and John's question (10.35-45)

And despite Jesus' clear teaching, his disciples – two of them, anyway – get it wrong yet again.

James and John want top places in Jesus' Kingdom. If you were invited to a meal, the most important guests would usually sit on the left and right hand sides of the host. The brothers may be thinking that Jesus is going to Jerusalem to set up a human kingdom, and they want good jobs in his government.

They have completely missed the point.

If the Son of Man must suffer, then the disciples must also be ready to suffer for others. They should not be squabbling over who gets the best jobs.

When Jesus asks the brothers, 'Can you drink the cup I drink or be baptized with the baptism I am baptized with?', they seem to think he is asking them if they have the guts to be as powerful as he is. Again, they are completely wrong:

The 'cup' here means suffering and death. In Old Testament times, if a king gave a banquet, he would hand a cup round to his guests. God was the true king of Israel. So a 'cup' became a symbol of what God hands out to people: blessing (Psalm 23.5) or punishment (Jeremiah 49.12). Christians must be ready to suffer. The word 'cup' here is paraphrased by the Good News Bible as 'cup of suffering'. This is the cup Jesus must drink (Mark 14.36).

The 'baptism' also means suffering and death, rather than the baptisms of John the Baptist or of the early Christians. The word 'baptism' literally means 'to be submerged', so here it means 'to be submerged in suffering'.

Jesus gives James and John what they ask for. They shall drink the same cup, and receive the same baptism. James was executed for his faith, loyal to the end (Acts 12.2). Strangely enough, there is very little evidence that John was also martyred; in fact, the evidence from the early Christian writers is that John went on to live to extreme old age. This is good evidence for the authenticity of Jesus' saying: no-one has tried to alter it to fit in with what actually happened to John.

Mark's first readers would have been reminded of their own Christian baptism and the 'cup' would have reminded them of the cup used at the Eucharist. Mark's Church may well have been persecuted; he is telling his readers what Christianity means: their faith meant that they had to be willing to die in Jesus' service.

But serving Jesus really means serving other people. Truly great people, says Jesus, are not egotists who want power. Instead, they give up their own interests to help others. Jesus does not have the right to give important places in the Kingdom as favours to his friends. God the Father has already decided. The most important people in the Kingdom are those who do most to help others –

> For even the Son of Man did not come to be served, but to serve, and to
> give his life as a ransom for many. Mark 10.45

(In English, 'many' implies 'lots but not all'. The Greek equivalent does not have this sense and can mean 'everybody'.)

Bartimaeus (10.46-52)

Only fifteen miles from Jerusalem, Jesus performs his final healing miracle in the Gospel. Yet it is the disciples, not Bartimaeus, who are really blind. They do not understand what being the Messiah means. Bartimaeus stands for those who do understand, and who genuinely follow Jesus.

Bartimaeus calls Jesus the 'Son of David', a synonym for 'Messiah';

it is interesting that Jesus does not tell him to be quiet. Mark may be making the point that you can call Jesus the Messiah (Son of David) when that means that he has to suffer. Here, Jesus is on the road to his death. The Messianic secrecy motif seems to fade from this point.

Bartimaeus 'followed Jesus on the road'. Mark's words may have a hidden meaning: it is Jesus' disciples who *follow him* (1.17, 1.18, 1.20, 2.14) on the *road* which is the *road to Jesus' death*. Every disciple must be like Bartimaeus, ready to follow Jesus on the road, even if it means facing death.

To consider:

'Those who are regarded as rulers of the Gentiles lord it over them... Not so with you.' If I lead others, in what spirit do I do so?

Day 27

Mark 11.1-11: The triumphal entry

This section begins Mark's account of the last week of Jesus' life, his passion narrative.

The events of Jesus' suffering and death, and his preparations for it, have always been crucial for Christianity. The cross is the main theme in the earliest Christian documents, Paul's letters. It's likely that the account of the passion was fixed very early in the oral tradition and that there were written versions as well.

Mark is likely, though this is not certain, to be basing his passion narrative on one of these written sources. If so, he takes a break from his source after the story of Jesus' entry into the capital, adds in the other material he has about Jerusalem, and returns to his source for chapter 14 onwards. (The first three Gospels – the synoptics, as they're called – have only one visit of Jesus to Jerusalem during his ministry; John suggests several, which is more likely historically. The Jerusalem material has to go somewhere and this is the most logical place for Mark to put it.) Mark takes from his source the precise timings which appear in his passion narrative, which are not found elsewhere in the Gospel (11.11, 11.20, 14.1, 14.12. 15.1, 15.33-34, 15.42). He does not follow his source slavishly and clearly edits it. If Mark's passion is compared to the other Gospels', it is much starker: Jesus goes to his death utterly alone and his suffering is emphasised by Mark even more than by the other evangelists. It may well be that he wants to emphasise the loneliness of Jesus' death; there are characters more sympathetic to Jesus in the other Gospels. Perhaps Mark has suppressed any material like this that he found in his source.

The entry into Jerusalem would have reminded Mark's original readers of Zechariah's words about the Messiah:

Rejoice, rejoice, people of Zion!
Shout for joy, you people of Jerusalem!
Look, your king is coming to you!
He comes triumphant and victorious, and riding on a donkey –
on a colt, the foal of a donkey...
Your king will make peace among the nations;
he will rule from sea to sea. (Zechariah 9.9, 10b)

Jesus seems deliberately to have chosen to fulfil this prophecy. He doesn't just come across a colt: he sent his disciples to fetch one he already knew was there. As Mark does not record a previous visit to Jerusalem, he probably thought Jesus' knowledge about the colt was a miracle. Interesting, too, that Jesus is found at the Mount of Olives; the Jewish historian Josephus said the Messiah was expected to appear there.

There are several things to note about the story:

1. The colt has never been ridden on before (verse 2). Any animal used in a Jewish religious ceremony had to be kept especially for that purpose. Jesus' entry into Jerusalem is therefore something sacred.

2. Victorious kings used to ride war horses in great processions but Jesus rides on a colt. He has come in peace.

3. The people shout the normal greeting for any pilgrim arriving in Jerusalem: 'Hosanna! [This originally meant something like 'Save us now!'] Blessed is he who comes in the name of the Lord!' (Psalm 118:26). But Mark says that they added something else. 'Blessed is the coming kingdom of our father David!' The people have heard Jesus teaching about the Kingdom of God, and now he has entered Jerusalem as the Messiah the prophets spoke about.

4. Jesus' actions must have taken great courage. The crowds welcomed him as the Messiah, but Jerusalem was where his opponents were most influential. A public display like this was very dangerous.

5. Jesus can act openly as the Messiah – what he does directly fulfils a Messianic prophecy – when it is linked to his suffering and death. The meaning of his messiahship is now clear and the time for the messianic secret has passed.

To consider:

Jesus' actions here took courage and humility. How good am I at being courageous and at being humble rather than proud?

Day 28

Mark 11.12-33: The judgement of Israel

The prophets in the Old Testament frequently proclaimed that God was outraged by the people of Israel. They had abandoned true faith, which included treating other people with compassion. In its place, they had opted for selfishness and, as far as religion was concerned, just going through the motions. The prophets warned people that God knew what they were doing and was going to punish them. This was his judgement on their crimes.

Mark shows Jesus, like the prophets before him, announcing God's judgement of Israel. We then have an example of the authorities' reaction.

The story of the cleansing of the Temple has been sandwiched by between the two halves of the cursing of the fig tree. (Mark likes this literary arrangement: he's used it before, in the story of Jairus' daughter and the woman with the haemorrhages (5.21-43).) For our purposes, it's easiest to consider them separately.

The cursing of the fig tree (11.12-14 and 20-26)

This is the last of the nature miracles. The prophets sometimes used the fig tree as a symbol of Israel (e.g. Jeremiah 8.13, Micah 7.1-6); this is the key to the meaning of the story.

The fig tree looks good, but there's nothing really there:
- Jesus is hungry and looks for figs; God is 'hungry' for the 'fruit' of good actions and right religion;
- It is not the right time for figs – or to look for the 'fruit' that God wants;
- No one will ever eat from the tree again; the old Israel is at an end, replaced by the Kingdom, the new people of God.

The people's religion looks good, but only on the surface. God looks deeper. Good actions, as well as genuine closeness to God, are part of religion. Otherwise, religion is useless.

Many people, including many Christians, don't like the story of the cursing of the fig tree. They'd say it is out of character for Jesus: it's destructive and unfair. On the other hand, the Old Testament prophets sometimes acted out their teachings (e.g. Jeremiah 27), so maybe this is what Jesus is doing.

Or perhaps Jesus originally told a parable about a fig tree, which meant the same as Mark's story. (The parable may have been the one in Luke 13.6-9, or something like it.) This has been changed from a parable *by* Jesus into a story *about* him.

Or perhaps we're being too picky. Maybe you can't apply modern preferences to the first century: we may be ultra-Green but they weren't. Destroying a tree for fuel or for its wood would have been fine. Are we just being sentimental?

At the end of the story, we have some teachings about prayer and faith, which may originally have been given by Jesus on another occasion. We can make a few comments:

- The idea of people moving mountains was a figure of speech used in the first century; it meant overcoming problems in life that seemed impossible to face. Jesus says people can do this, if they have true faith.

- People will receive what they ask for when they pray. God will always answer prayer (even though the way he answers it will not necessarily be the way people expect).

- People have to forgive others when they pray. If they do not, they cannot receive God's forgiveness for their sins. (This is like the Lord's Prayer – see Matthew 6.9-15.)

The cleansing of the Temple (11.15-19)

When the Messiah came, people thought he would go to the Temple to ensure it was only used for the true worship of God (Malachi 3.1, Zechariah 14.21). This is what Jesus does. As the Temple was central to Judaism, Jesus' actions show God's judgement on Israel. Jesus says the people had turned the house of prayer into a bandits' den (Jeremiah 7.11, Isaiah 56.7).

Traders were selling the things required for the sacrifices and rituals: wine, oil, birds and other animals. These were required for the sacrifices. Jesus arrives at the Temple near Passover time, when it was crowded with pilgrims. It was impractical for them all to bring their own sacrificial animals. Moreover, such animals had to be in perfect condition physically. Scenting an opportunity to make a fast buck, the traders had moved in. They were making a fat profit and people were being exploited.

Every year, male Jews had to pay a tax of half a shekel (about two days' average pay) to keep the Temple going. The tax was due at Passover time. The Jewish pilgrims came from many different countries and the money-changers exchanged their foreign currency for the special Temple coinage needed for the tax. The money changers, too, were making a fortune.

People were using the Temple as a short cut between the Mount of Olives and the eastern part of Jerusalem.

Jesus was appalled. The Temple was for the worship of God; it was not a convenient short cut or an easy opportunity to relieve people of their money. There was something else, too. All these things were going on in the Court of the Gentiles. This was the only part of the Temple where non-Jews were allowed. The Temple was not just has house of prayer for the Jews, but for 'all peoples': Gentiles. The traders obviously didn't think this mattered very much. Jesus did.

And his words were not just an attack on the businessmen. He was also speaking against the Jewish leaders, who allowed such things to go on.

'What right have you to do these things?' (11.27-33)

The chief priests, scribes and elders were probably sent by the Sanhedrin, the Jewish council. One of its duties was to look after religious affairs. The delegation is looking for a way to trap Jesus. If he says his authority comes from God, they can arrest him for blasphemy. If he says he is acting on his own authority – doing what *he* thinks is right – they've got him again; no sane person would claim the right to do what he did in the Temple of God.

And Jesus avoids the trap, asking them a question instead. Where did John get his right to baptise from? God, or people?

Now the Jewish leaders can't win. If they say John was acting on his own, they risk a riot. People could overhear them, and the general view was that John was genuinely sent by God. Moreover, John did not just baptise people; he also said, 'After me, someone more powerful is coming. I am not good enough to get down and undo his sandals' (1.7). John pointed to Jesus.

If they say John's authority came from God, Jesus could quite reasonably ask why they didn't believe what John said.

Their only escape is to say, 'We do not know.' As they will not answer Jesus, Jesus will not answer them. They refuse to see what is staring them in the face: Jesus, like John, gets his authority from God.

To consider:

True religion can never be a matter of appearances.

106

Day 29

Mark 12.1-12: The allegory of the vineyard

This is another parable, but rather a different one. For a start, it's really about the Jewish authorities, rather than directly about the Kingdom of God. Also, it's an *allegory*: every person in the story represents a real person; every event represents a real event. So it's rather more complex than most parables, which only make one point. However, Jesus once again draws his imagery from agriculture. In Galilee, foreigners often bought land and rented it to the locals, who farmed it for them. The Galileans often didn't like it: the land of Israel belonged to them, not to foreigners, and they weren't going to put up with it.

The meaning of the parable of the vineyard is as follows:

– The vineyard owner is God and the vineyard is Israel. Jesus borrows the imagery from the Old Testament: the prophet Isaiah also told a story about a vineyard. Isaiah's story ended like this:

> Israel is the vineyard of the LORD almighty…
> He expected them to do what was good,
> but instead they committed murder.
> He expected them to do what was right,
> but their victims cried out for justice. (Isaiah 5.7)

In both Isaiah's and Jesus' parables, the people of Israel ignore what God wants.

– The tenants are the people of Israel, especially the authorities.
– The servants are the Old Testament prophets, the messengers of God. (The Greek word for 'servant' can also mean 'slave', which is how some translations render it.) God and the vineyard owner both want something: God wants the people to do good and the vineyard owner wants his share of the harvest. So they both send messengers to the people, but they're ignored.
– The servants are beaten or killed; the people treated the prophets in the same way. The Letter to the Hebrews describes the treatment of the prophets like this:

> Some were mocked and whipped, and others were put in chains and taken off to prison. They were stoned, they were sawn in two, they were killed by the sword. They went round in the skins of sheep or goats – poor, persecuted and ill-treated. (Hebrews 11.36-37)

- The vineyard owner / God decides to send his son. If the people will not listen to the messengers, they might listen to him. The story talks about the man's 'beloved son', the phrase used by the voice from heaven at the baptism and Transfiguration (Mark 1.11, 9.7).
- The tenants kill the man's son; the Jewish leaders will kill Jesus.
- The owner of the vineyard will kill the tenants. God will not allow the Jewish leaders to get away with killing Jesus. The destruction of the Temple in AD 70 may have been thought of by the early Christians as this punishment.
- The owner will hand the vineyard over to others. The vineyard is Israel, God's people, and the 'others' are the outcasts, the tax collectors, sinners and Gentiles. God's people are not just the Jews. We have seen already how Jesus stressed the inclusion of the outsiders in the Kingdom.
- At the end of the allegory, Jesus quotes Psalm 118 from the Old Testament. Again, what he says has a hidden meaning: builders do not think a lump of rock is suitable for use as a building stone, but this is what it turns out to be. And people do not think a carpenter from Nazareth is really the Messiah, but this is what he turns out to be.

The chief priests, scribes and elders understand what the allegory means, and they are incensed. The crowd at the moment still thinks a great deal of Jesus; the authorities' fear of the crowd means all they can do for now is wait. But they will make a move soon.

To consider:

Do we always listen to what God wants?

Day 30:

Mark 12.13-27: Life in this world, and the next

The question about paying taxes (12.13-17)

The Pharisees and Herodians were sent to Jesus, presumably by the Sanhedrin. At first, they try to lull him into a false sense of security by being smarmy, but he sees straight through it. The question they ask is whether Jews should pay the Roman Empire's taxes or not.

The people of Israel hated paying those taxes, and with good reason. It wasn't just that they were very high, though that was bad enough; they were a constant reminder that Israel was an occupied country. In AD 6, when the tax was first imposed in Israel, there had been an uprising led by a Zealot called Judas of Galilee. So the tax made people very angry. It was paid in Roman coinage, stamped with a picture of Caesar – and this was against the Torah, which did not allow images (Deuteronomy 4.16). And in any case, the real king of Israel was God, not some foreign tyrant.

The Pharisees and Herodians put Jesus in a very difficult position. If he says people should pay up, he will lose all credibility. No Messiah would support paying taxes to Rome. If he says they shouldn't pay, the Romans could arrest him as a traitor.

Once again, Jesus' reply is very shrewd: 'Pay Caesar what belongs to Caesar – and God what belongs to God.'

In the first century, coins were officially the property of the ruler who issued them. The denarius, the coin they show Jesus, bears the image of Caesar. Human beings bear the image of God (Genesis 1.27). If people pay tax, they are only giving Caesar what he owns. Yet people owe much more to God than they do to Caesar. Caesar's kingdom will pass away; God's Kingdom will not.

This brings us to a question: how should all this be applied by Christians today?

It is often said that Christians – and religious people in general – should keep their noses out of politics. The two don't mix: politics is about this world and religion is about the next. Religious people should mind their own business and leave politics to the professionals.

It will probably not amaze you that the people who say things like this tend to be politicians.

The problem with this view is that religion is actually very political. True religion teaches that people should be treated with love, compassion and sympathy, concepts which some politicians find a nuisance. Other politicians are actually inspired by their own faith: they genuinely want to serve other people, and try to put this into practice in public office. All three major political parties – Labour, Conservative and the Liberal Democrats – owe a great deal in their ideas to Christianity.

Moreover, if you believe God is a God of justice, who demands that people be looked after and treated well, religious people cannot help but criticise the political process. Politics is too important to be left to the politicians. The Churches in the UK frequently criticise the government if they feel it has strayed too far from Christian ideals. Margaret Thatcher's Conservative government was heavily criticised by the Churches for not doing enough to help the poor. Tony Blair's Labour government was heavily criticised by the Churches for the Iraq war.

Most voters in the UK, including Christians, vote the way their parents did, without thinking much about it, or don't bother voting at all. But perhaps this isn't good enough. The ideal is probably for Christians to look at the programmes of all the political parties, apply a fairly large pinch of salt, and vote for the one who best seems to support Christian teaching, especially on caring for others – and not just others in the UK, but in the rest of the world.

As far as taxes are concerned, it's probably a Christian's duty to pay them, though some would say the exception is when they're being used for immoral purposes. Tax evasion is dishonest, and Christians should be honest.

Many early Christians felt they had to be good citizens, to obey the authorities. This view appears in St Paul's letter to the Romans, where he says that governments are appointed by God (Romans 13.1-7). This teaching was gleefully pounced on by the Nazis, who said Christians had to obey them because they had God on their side. But Paul was writing for a specific situation; he was trying to persuade his readers to keep their heads down, to avoid becoming targets for persecution. He was not writing for today, and it's hard to imagine his supporting governments who practise evil. Many Christians opposed Hitler, though too many supported him.

So Christians' involvement in politics, like their involvement in anything else, should be informed by the ideals of Christianity.

The question about the resurrection (12.18-27)

Most Jews in the time of Jesus believed in life after death: God would bring all the dead back to life, some time in the future. He would judge them, send the wicked to hell, and welcome the good into heaven. This idea was called 'the resurrection of the dead'.

There was an exception, though. The Sadducees rejected all belief in life after death.

The Sadducees were from the priestly families in Jerusalem. They only accepted ideas that were in the Torah, and the Torah did not mention life after death. This is the basis of their dispute with Jesus.

The parable they tell is based on a law in Deuteronomy 25.5-6. This says that if a married man dies and there are no children, his brother must marry the widow, so that the dead man's family line will continue.

Suppose, they say, there are seven brothers. The first one marries the woman, has no children, and dies. The second one does the same. So does the third one. Eventually, all seven have married her. If there is life after death, they say, who will be the woman's husband when they meet again? From the Sadducees' point of view, the whole thing seems daft. They think it is much easier to say there is no life after death.

This is the kind of argument about the Torah the rabbis had. Jesus says the Sadducees simply do not understand God's power, and have misinterpreted the scriptures.

Many thought that life after death would be very much like life on earth. Jesus is saying if you understand the new life properly, there is no problem. There will be no marriage; instead, people will be 'like the angels in heaven'. What Jesus is saying is that the new life will be very different from this one.

The Sadducees only accepted the Torah, so Jesus points them to another section of it. In the book Moses (Exodus), one passage does suggest there is life after death. In Exodus 3, God speaks to Moses from the burning bush, saying, 'I am the God of Abraham, the God of Isaac, and the God of Jacob.' By Moses' time, all three were long dead. But God says 'I am' their God, not 'I was'. So they must somehow still be alive.

Notes

When Jesus refers back to the Torah, he says, 'in the book of Moses, in the account of the bush', rather than 'Exodus 3.6'. This was the way people referred to Biblical references in those days. The chapter and verse numbers were added to the text much later, so you referred to a passage by a keyword or phrase.

'Exodus' is the Greek, not the Hebrew name for the book.

Incidentally, it was much less easy to look up passages in the Torah then than it is now. We can just find the right page; they had to work through a scroll, rolling and unrolling it until they came to the section they wanted. And there were no sub-headings, chapter or verse numbers, or even spaces between words to help. Knowing the scriptures represented a great deal of hard work and an enormous feat of memory.

To consider:

'Pay Caesar what belongs to Caesar – and God what belongs to God.'

Day 31

Mark 12.28-44: Further teaching

The greatest commandment (12.28-34)

One scribe was very impressed by Jesus' answers to the Jewish leaders' questions, and decided to ask his professional opinion on a professional problem.

The scribes or rabbis calculated that the Torah contained over 600 commandments. This was without counting in the Pharisees' 'fence around the Law', which added thousands of footnotes. Rabbis debated which of the Torah's commandments were the most important of them all.

The reply Jesus gives is unique; it's highly likely that he was the first rabbi to summarise the Torah in this way.

The first commandment – to love God – comes from Deuteronomy 6.4-5. It begins the prayer called the *Shema*, which opens synagogue services. The second – 'love your neighbour as yourself' – comes from Leviticus 19.18.

The scribe agrees with Jesus: loving God and loving your neighbour is more important even than worship in the Jewish Temple. For some Jews, such as the Sadducees, *nothing* was more important than that. What Jesus says is radical, not commonplace.

The question about the Messiah (12.35-37)

This section of Mark ends Jesus' teaching in the Temple. He stops answering questions and starts asking them instead.

Jesus is asking whether the Messiah has to be the 'Son of David' – descended from King David – as well. He quotes Psalm 110, which was attributed to David himself. There, David seems to say that the Messiah is his Lord: hardly something you'd call your descendant.

All this may mean that Jesus was actually not descended from King David after all, and he was defending himself. The Messiah need not be the Son of David as well. The problem with this view is that there is plenty of New Testament evidence that Jesus *was* David's descendant.

Or Jesus may mean that the Messiah is not going to be anything like his ancestor. He's David's Lord, not a son who follows in his footsteps. David may have been a military leader and a statesman but the Messiah is not going to be. The Messiah may be David's descendant but that's where the resemblance ends.

The scribes (12.38-40)

Matthew and Luke have much longer versions of Jesus' warnings about the scribes (Matthew 23, Luke 11.37-52). Many were genuinely good men, but others were two faced: hypocrites who pretended to be religious but who were only interested in themselves.

The 'long robes' they like to wear may mean the talliths, garments which were usually only put on for prayer: the scribes ostentatiously wore them all the time. Or the Greek can mean they 'like to walk about in porticoes', the covered walkways in the Temple where the rabbis taught. Whichever is right, they like to be noticed and want people to look up to them. They insist on the best seats at synagogues and at dinner parties. They make a big show of praying but extort money from needy people.

The widow's offering (12.41-44)

Jesus has just been talking about the scribes' attitude to widows. Now, Mark tells a story about one. (The key word 'widow' may have been the link which he used to bring together two originally separate stories.)

The Temple's treasury was used for the daily sacrifices and running costs. The coins the widow gave were worth a quadrans: 1/64th of a denarius, a day's pay for a labourer.

Some scholars wonder how Jesus knew how much people gave. So they suggest this was originally a parable told by Jesus, which was later changed into a story about him.

The point, however, remains the same. The best gift is not something you can afford, but something you cannot afford.

To consider:

'Love the Lord your God with all your heart and with all your soul and with all your might and with all your strength.'
'Love your neighbour as yourself.'

Day 32

Mark 13: The apocalypse of Mark

People in Jesus' time were very interested in the issues of death, judgement and the end of the world. There was a whole genre of literature which dealt with them: *apocalyptic writing* or *apocalypses*. 'Apocalyptic' comes from a Greek word meaning 'to uncover' or 'to reveal'; supposedly, the secrets of God were revealed.

Apocalyptic literature was tremendously popular in the centuries around Jesus' time; enormous numbers of apocalypses, both Jewish and Christian, were written. Two examples have found their way into the Bible: Daniel, in the Old Testament, and the book of Revelation in the New.

For present day readers, apocalyptic books read very oddly and can seem very dated. They were usually written for people who were being persecuted or suffering oppression, and they contrasted the dreadful present situation with what would happen in the future. God would triumph in the end and his people would be saved.

Apocalypses often claim to be visions or dreams given by God to the writer. They use extreme, even grotesque, imagery and coded language. There are number codes, monstrous beats and weird happenings, which all represented things that were really going on in the world. The book of Revelation, for example, is really about the persecution of Christians by the Romans in the first century, and the imagery used is very graphic. To get a flavour of apocalyptic, have a glance at Revelation, especially chapter 13.

In some ways, Mark 13 is similar to apocalyptic; indeed, it's sometimes called the *Little Apocalypse*. It is, however, nothing like as extreme as apocalyptic literature. There are no monsters or number symbolism; nor does it describe the writer's visions or dreams: Jesus' authority is enough. Apocalyptic's coded language often sets out a timetable for when God is going to act; Mark 13 doesn't, and actually discourages people from trying to work one out.

Christians believe Jesus will return at the end of time and will judge people. In Mark 13, the idea seems to be that the Kingdom of God will finally and fully arrive with the return of Jesus – but when that will be, no-one knows. Some Christians take the descriptions of Jesus' return literally: the Son of Man really will descend from the sky on a cloud. Others would see this as imagery and say that Jesus will come back, but we don't know exactly what this will be like. (The technical term for the second coming of Jesus is the *parousia*.)

As you read through it, you'll probably agree with the assessment that Mark 13 is the most difficult chapter in the Gospel. It's also confused: it sometimes seems to say that the end will be soon (verses 28-30); at other times, the timing of the end cannot be calculated. What sources Mark was using is unclear; how much – if any – goes back to Jesus himself is also unclear. Apocalypses were often said to be written by religious heroes such as Moses, Enoch or others. It would not be surprising if an author claimed an apocalypse he'd written was actually uttered by Jesus.

A middle view is to say that there are some genuine sayings of Jesus in the chapter (13.2 is usually taken to be one, for example). These have been worked up by some Christian writer, writing before Mark, into this longer speech.

We can, though, offer the following comments:

1. The Temple actually *was* destroyed in AD 70 by the Romans.

2. Lots of people will claim to be Jesus, but they will be impostors. This may have happened in the early Church. Certainly, other people were thought to be the Messiah; one example is Bar Kochba, who led a rebellion against Rome in AD 135. And in modern times, leaders of cults often claim to be Christ himself.

3. There will be wars, famines or earthquakes, but they are like the early contractions before childbirth. A child can be born very quickly after the first contractions or the birth can be much later. Christians should not get carried away by such things as wars: Jesus may not arrive for a long time. Many early Christians expected the parousia to be very soon. For most Christians today, the parousia is something that will happen in the far future.

4. The idea that families will be broken up is a common feature of apocalyptic. Here, Christianity will split families.

5. Before the end comes, everyone in the world must hear the gospel. Passages like these drive Christian missionary work.

6. Anyone who holds out through persecution – the sort of persecution Mark's Church was going through – will be saved.

7. What 'the desolating sacrilege' of verse 14 means is unclear. (The words can be translated as 'the abomination of desolation'.) Mark expected 'the reader' to know this already. It may refer to an attempt by the Emperor Caligula to set up his statue in the Temple in AD 40. It may refer to the Antichrist: the Devil or his representative, whom some people expected to arrive at the end of the world. Luke replaces this verse with a reference to Jerusalem's destruction in AD 70 by the Romans. This is perhaps the best explanation of 'the desolating sacrilege'. It also makes sense of the

rest of verses 14 to 17, which seem to describe escaping before a siege.

8. The parable of the fig tree (verses 28-31) seems to suggest the end is very close. This is contradicted by Jesus' saying 'But of that day or that hour no one knows, not even the angels in heaven, nor the Son, but only the Father.' No apocalyptic writer would have said this. It may reflect Mark's use of different sources. Whatever is the case, the passage is confused.

9. Jesus' followers must be on their guard because they do not know when he will return. People should live every day as though it is their last, as if they could at any moment be judged by God.

10. Jesus and his message will stand for ever:

Heaven and earth will pass away,
but my words will not pass away.   (13.31)

To consider:

Whatever we think about the timing of the second coming, it has been suggested that we should live as though it is today that Christ will return to judge us.

Day 33

Mark 14.1-11: The last act begins

Mark 14.1 begins with one of the precise timings that run through the passion narrative: 'It was two days before the Passover and the festival of Unleavened Bread.' These used to be two separate festivals, but they had been combined by the time of Jesus. Passover remembered the Jews' escape from Egypt. The festival of Unleavened Bread lasted for seven days afterwards and marked the beginning of the barley harvest. The name reminded the Jews that when God brought them out of Egypt, there was no time for the bread to rise. ('Leaven' more or less means 'yeast', though strictly speaking, it's a lump of risen dough, saved from the last time you bake, which is then put in the new batch. It wasn't so easy then to separate the yeast from the dough.)

It was spring, and Jerusalem was packed. So were the neighbouring villages. Every Jew wanted to spend at least one Passover in Jerusalem. As a result, thousands of people were jammed into the city, which was only the size of a small town by today's standards. The Romans had the usual problems of crowd control, but it was a powder keg too. Patriotic feelings were at fever pitch. The crowds would be thinking about God's saving them from foreign oppression: not from the Egyptians this time, but from the Romans. Would God intervene? Had the Messiah arrived and was he ready to lead them?

It was also difficult for the Sanhedrin. The Jewish council wanted to keep the Romans sweet, but with Jerusalem full of excitable pilgrims, anything could happen. Arresting Jesus openly would be too risky. The Romans were not gentle when it came to putting down riots. However, Judas offers them an opportunity.

Why did Judas betray Jesus? We don't really know. Mark may be suggesting he did it for the money. Film versions of the life of Jesus usually make Judas a sympathetic character, suggesting that he was trying to help Jesus in some way, perhaps by putting Jesus in a situation where he has to declare openly that the is the Messiah. Again, it's an interesting idea, but there's no evidence. Luke says Judas was possessed by the Devil (Luke 22.3). It may be that Judas was a Zealot. The name 'Iscariot' may be linked to a word for 'dagger bearer' and we know Jesus had Zealot disciples, like Simon the Zealot and perhaps James and John. If this is right, then Judas may have lost patience with Jesus when he finally realized Jesus was not going to be a military, Zealot Messiah, and Judas turned him in. But this is only a possibility; the evidence is very thin. We just don't know.

The evangelists aren't sympathetic to Judas at all; the man who betrayed the Son of God is depicted as wholly unsympathetic. Indeed, the later the Gospel, the nastier the characterisation of Judas. (For example, in John's account of the anointing of Jesus, it's Judas who complains about the waste of money, and John says Judas is a liar: he doesn't care about the poor because he's a thief (John 12.4-6).)

The Anointed One is finally anointed

As we have seen, 'Messiah' and 'Christ' both mean 'the Anointed One': the king, who was anointed at his coronation. The problem is that the Anointed One hasn't been anointed. There's a sense in which this could just about be said to have happened: the baptism of Jesus was a bit like an anointing, but it was done with water and not oil.

But the Messiah, the King, has to be anointed. The Jews expected Elijah, the greatest prophet of them all, to do this. Instead, it's just an ordinary person, and a woman at that: very much a second-class citizen in the first century. Luke hints she was a prostitute (Luke 7.36-50). It's not done in a palace, but in the house on a leper, an outcast.

So, the Messiah is anointed, not at the beginning of his work, but at the end of it, on the way to his death. This is what the Messiah's mission is, and it's only when he's facing death that Jesus openly admits to being the Messiah (14.62). And the anointing is not carried out by a religious hero, but by a woman as ordinary as the people Jesus mixed with every day.

The anointing is not just about confirming Jesus' identity; it's about his death. The bodies of the dead were anointed as part of the funeral arrangements. Bizarrely, it's as though the funeral rites are carried out on someone who's still alive – but whose coming death is an absolute certainty.

So the king is anointed, and the king is about to die.

To consider:

Do I ever betray Jesus?

119

Day 34

Mark 14.12-26: The Last Supper

Jesus is going to die. This is the last time he eats with his disciples.

Perhaps Jesus had arranged about the room before he sends the disciples out, or perhaps Mark thinks his knowledge is a miracle. As water jugs would usually have been carried by women, a man carrying one would be very noticeable. This suggests a pre-arranged sign.

Mark says the Last Supper was also a Passover meal. The Passover is still one of the most important festivals of Judaism; it recalls how God brought his people out of Egypt and saved them from slavery. Today's Passover celebration grew out of the sort of festival celebrated every year in Jerusalem in Jesus' time.

The Passover meal was eaten in the evening, at the beginning (sunset) of 15th Nisan, the Jewish Passover day. At the centre of the meal was the Passover lamb. During the afternoon, the head of the family took it to the Temple, where it was killed as a sacrifice. Its blood was thrown against the altar by the priests, and the carcass was handed back to be taken home. This recalled the first Passover in Egypt, when the blood of the lamb was daubed on the doorposts of the Israelite homes, and the Angel of Death passed over them, but killed the first born sons of the Egyptians (Exodus 12.21-28). The lamb was eaten with other symbolic foods, including bread and wine.

Jesus predicts his betrayal, but as far as we can see, the other disciples did not suspect Judas. 'The Son of Man will go just as it is written about him'; Jesus knows his death will not be some sort of wasteful tragedy; God had spoken of it in the Scriptures.

Jesus goes on to say that it would have been better for his betrayer if he had never been born. Later Christian writers have generally taken this to mean that Judas will go to hell. Or it may refer to Judas' suicide, recorded by Matthew (27.5). Perhaps Jesus meant it would have been better for Judas never to have been born than to suffer the terrible shame and guilt that drove him to this.

The new covenant

God's saving the Jewish people from Egypt showed his special relationship – the *covenant* – with them. Mark believes the Last Supper to be a new Passover meal, celebrating the *new* covenant. Jesus is going to make this new covenant with his death.

Jesus is going to die. He takes the bread, says a prayer of thanks to

God, and breaks it: exactly as the head of a Jewish family did at every Passover meal. But Jesus adds something: the bread is his body. Just as the bread was broken at the Passover meal, Jesus' body is going to be broken on the cross.

The wine at the Passover meal symbolised the promises God made with the Jews. Jesus takes a cup and again gives thanks in the usual way. But then he says something else that is entirely new: 'This is my blood of the covenant, which is poured out for many.' When Moses sealed God's first covenant, he took the blood from the animal sacrifices and threw it on the people, saying, 'This is the blood that seals the covenant which the LORD made with you' (Exodus 24.8). The prophet Jeremiah, living when things had gone badly wrong for the Jews and they were in exile in Babylon, wrote:

> The LORD says:
> 'The time is coming when I shall make a new covenant with the people of Israel... I will forgive their sins. (Jeremiah 31.31, 34)

We can, then, make the following points:
1. Jesus says that the wine is his *blood which seals God's (new) covenant.* The Passover lamb was sacrificed, and Jesus will be sacrificed. The promises have been fulfilled; the new covenant has begun.
2. The Passover was God's great saving act. The death and resurrection of Jesus will be God's second, greater saving act. The sacrifices of the old covenant are replaced by and fulfilled in Jesus' death and the Passover lamb is replaced by the Eucharist.
3. When Christians eat and drink at the Eucharist, they are members of God's new covenant.

But this will not all go on for ever. Jesus says, 'I will not drink again of the fruit of the vine until that day when I drink it anew in the Kingdom of God' (verse 25). One of the images of the Kingdom of God was the Messianic banquet, the banquet given by the Messiah. Mark wants his readers to understand that the Eucharist is a *foretaste* or *promise* of the banquet they will share with Jesus in heaven. That banquet, like the Eucharist, has been made possible by Jesus' death and resurrection.

To consider:

Jesus said, 'If you eat my flesh and drink my blood, you live in me – and I live in you.' (John 6.56)

121

In more detail...

The Eucharist in Christianity today

'Mark in 40 Days' is really a book about the Gospel. So why have a section on this?

The Eucharist – the act of worship that re-enacts the Last Supper – was intended to be a sign of the unity of all Christians. However, since the days of the early Church, Christianity divided into the different Christian denominations; disagreements about the meaning of the Eucharist and how is should be celebrated were often at the heart of this. We're now living in an age when ecumenism and co-operation between Christians characterise the relations between them; the old bitterness, mutual denunciations and, yes, hatred are fading. Sadly, they have not faded away altogether.

In helping to build bridges, it's important to know what our fellow Christians actually believe. That can sweep away myths, half truths and misunderstandings.

The present writers do not propose any solutions as to how the Churches should draw together. But this section is offered to deepen understanding, as an important first step towards the unity which Christ desired for his followers (John 17, especially verses 20-21).

The Eucharist today

Almost all Christians re-enact the Last Supper in a service; the name most Christians would accept for this type of service is the *Eucharist*, which comes from a Greek word meaning 'to give thanks'. So, 'Eucharist' means 'thanksgiving'.

Different Christians have different names for the Eucharist:

– The Mass (Roman Catholics, and some Anglicans: i.e. members of the Church of England, Church of Wales, Church of Ireland and the other Anglican Churches throughout the world);

– Holy Communion (Anglicans and Methodists);

– The Lord's Supper (Anglicans and some Protestants);

– The Liturgy (Orthodox);

– The Breaking of Bread (a name found in the New Testament (Acts 2.42), used by the Brethren and some other Protestants)

It has to be said that behind these different names are very different views of what the Eucharist is, and what it's for. Arguments about the Eucharist were a main cause of the Reformation, when the Protestant Churches split off from the Catholic Church in the sixteenth Century.

Beliefs about the real presence

At the Last Supper, Jesus took bread and wine, shared them among his disciples, and told them to repeat his actions. Jesus said the bread was his body, and the wine was his blood. (The point in the Eucharist at which Christians receive the bread and wine, as Jesus told them to do, is the *communion*.)

For Christians, the key question about the Eucharist is: *What happens to the bread and wine?*

Jesus said the bread was his body, and the wine was his blood. So,

-   Did Jesus mean that they changed into his body and blood?
-   Or was he using picture language (imagery)?

For most of Christian history, Christians have taken Jesus literally. This may sound surprising, but the majority of Christians have always believed that the bread at the Eucharist does become Jesus' body, and the wine does become Jesus' blood. Some scholars think this belief is even found in the New Testament, though others argue equally strongly that it isn't there at all. (See 1 Corinthians 11.23-29 and John 6.48-58. What do you think?)

So, most Christians believe that Jesus himself is *really present* in the bread and the wine. The name given to this idea is the doctrine of the *real presence*.

Different Christians who believe in the real presence have different ways of understanding it.

All this needs careful scrutiny.

One way to help understand the doctrine of the real presence is to use a parallel – an analogy. Think about this:

On a sunny day, sunlight could be said to be 'everywhere'. (We know it's not absolutely everywhere, but let's allow it for the sake of the analogy.) Yet you can focus the sunlight – concentrate it in one place – perhaps by using a magnifying glass. In fact, you can focus the sunlight so much that it can start a fire.

God is omnipresent – everywhere. Christians believe Jesus is God, so Jesus can be said to be everywhere. Yet, just as the sunlight's presence can be focussed in one place, so Jesus' presence can be focussed in one place. Where? In the bread and in the wine.

Christians who believe in the real presence say that this 'focussing' of Jesus' presence takes place when the priest or minister repeats Jesus' words over the bread and wine. In the Eucharist, the priest or minister reads aloud an account of the Last Supper. This includes the words 'This is my body' and 'This is my blood'.

In the time of Jesus, 'my body' meant 'myself'. In the same way, 'my blood' meant 'myself'. It's a misunderstanding to think that the bread becomes Jesus' corpse, or that the wine becomes Jesus' blood plasma, red and white blood cells and haemoglobin. It is believed that *both bread and wine become Jesus himself.*

Eating the 'bread' and drinking the 'wine' enable Christians to have a genuine meeting with the risen Jesus himself.

The risen Jesus is present in the same way in the bread as in the wine. (For this reason, Roman Catholics sometimes only receive the 'bread' – they communicate 'in one kind'. This custom developed about 1000 years ago. It is much less common now, although it still happens. Normally, though, Roman Catholics receive both 'bread' and 'wine'.)

Christians who believe in the real presence include:
-   Roman Catholics
-   The Orthodox
-   Some Anglicans (though not all)
-   Coptic (Egyptian) Christians
-   Lutherans

Some individual Christians within other Churches also believe in the real presence.

Looking deeper: transubstantiation

St Thomas Aquinas (1224 or 1225–1274) was one of the great philosophers of the Christian world. He said that Jesus becomes really present in the bread and wine by *transubstantiation*.

This is how it works.

Transubstantiation has to do with the question, 'What makes a thing what it is?' (We could ask, 'What makes a chair a chair?' or 'What makes me me'?)

The Greek philosopher Aristotle (384-322 BC) said that matter (stuff – physical things – anything that exists) was made up of two things:

-   *substance*: what something *really* is

– *accidents* – what something appears to be or *seems* to be. (Nothing to do with car crashes! This is a different use of the same word.) Accidents include:
   – what it looks like
   – what it smells like
   – what it tastes like
   – what it feels like
   – what it sounds like, and so on.
   – (We could add, 'What scientific analysis tells us it's like.')
Thomas Aquinas borrowed Aristotle's ideas about substance and accidents, and went on to say:
   In the Eucharist,
   – the substance of the bread and wine changes, but
   – the accidents of the bread and wine stay exactly the same.
So, it still looks, smells, tastes and feels like bread and wine. Come to that, if you ran lots of scientific tests on it, it would still *appear* to be bread and wine.
   But that is no longer what it is.
   In fact, it is the body and blood of Jesus – it is Jesus himself.

The Roman Catholic Church teaches that the bread and wine become Jesus himself through transubstantiation. This is also believed by some Anglicans.
   In fact, if you believe in transubstantiation, it's not correct to talk about 'bread' and 'wine' after the consecration. Despite appearances, they are no longer bread and wine.

Further Ideas

Martin Luther (1483-1546), the great German Protestant reformer, disliked the idea of transubstantiation, and called it an 'unnatural monster'.
   Luther proposed the doctrine of *consubstantiation:*
   – The substance of Christ's body and blood *is added to* the substance of the bread and wine.
   – So, they are *both* bread and wine *and* the body and blood of Christ.
This view of the real presence is held by some Anglicans. Modern Lutheran belief is also very similar. Note that as Lutherans are Protestants, it's a mistake to say Protestants do not believe in the real presence. Some do.
   Another Christian leader at the Reformation, Ulrich Zwingli (1484-

1531), who led the Reformation in Zurich, rejected all belief in the real presence. He could be said, in fact, to have taught a real *absence*.

Zwingli said:

- There is no change in the bread and wine. They stay bread and wine.
- When Jesus called the bread and wine his body and blood, he was using picture language – metaphor. The bread and wine *stand for* or *represent* Jesus' body and blood. (In modern terms, we might say a picture of a loved one stands for or represents them, but isn't really them. But they are very strong reminders of them.)

Zwingli noted that Jesus said at the Last Supper that his disciples should 'do this in remembrance of me' (1 Corinthians 11.24). Zwingli thought *this* was what the Eucharist was for: to remember Jesus, and everything he had done for humanity. The idea of the real presence was wrong, and was not the point anyway.

Many Protestant Churches, including the Free Churches, agree with Zwingli. So do some Anglicans.

During the Reformation in England, Thomas Cranmer (1489-1556) was Henry VIII's Archbishop of Canterbury. (Cranmer did the same job for Henry's son Edward VI, too. After Edward's death, Cranmer was executed by burning by Edward's half-sister Mary.)

Cranmer changed his mind many times about the real presence, not least because Henry VIII believed in transubstantiation and it was not a good idea to disagree with him. However, Cranmer did teach that, at the moment of communion – when the worshipper receives bread and wine – *Jesus becomes spiritually present to the believer.*

Some Anglicans today hold this view.

Some Christians who believe in the real presence say that there's little point in trying to tie the doctrine down as transubstantiation or consubstantiation. They would argue the real presence is something too great and extraordinary to put into words. The Orthodox, and some Anglicans, think like this.

Summing Up

We can put Christians' different views about the real presence on the following diagram:

Real presence   Real absence

Aquinas: Luther: Cranmer: Zwingli
transubstantiation   consubstantiation   spiritual presence

Roman Catholic   *Many Free Churches*

Orthodox: belief in
real presence but not
defined as transubstantiation
or consubstantiation

Anglicanism includes all these positions

There is a great deal more that could be said. We only have the space for a few more points:

— For Christians who believe that the Eucharist really is a meeting with the risen Jesus, it's the most important part of their worship. They are taught to go every Sunday and on major holy days. In the Roman Catholic Church (and in some Anglican churches), the Eucharist is celebrated every single day of the year, except Good Friday.

— The Eucharist is less important to Christians who do not believe in the real presence. Some Anglican churches do not have a Eucharist every Sunday, though they have other services instead. In some Protestant churches, it is celebrated once a month, or in some cases less frequently.

— Christians who believe in the real presence treat the 'bread' and 'wine' after the consecration with great respect. Any 'wine' left after communion is consumed, usually by the priest. Any 'bread' left is either consumed or is placed in a special cupboard in the church called a 'tabernacle'.

— Christians who believe in the real presence will often use the bread and wine to help to focus their worship in church:
    — They may genuflect – go down on one knee – to the tabernacle or to the host (the 'bread')
    — They may pray in front of the host. This happens, for example, on Maundy Thursday.

— The vessels holding the 'bread' and the 'wine' are called the chalice (cup) and the paten (plate) or ciborium (a vessel like a flattened goblet, which holds the host). They may be made of precious metal. They are carefully cleaned by the priest after communion.

- Churches which believe in the real presence often have rituals and 'equipment' which underline the importance of the Eucharist. These could include candles, incense, bells, and special clothes (vestments) for the priest. The table on which the bread and wine are placed in called the altar, and this is often richly decorated with coloured cloth or linen.

- The Mass is thought of as a sacrifice. This is because it connects back to the sacrifice of Jesus on the cross. It is not *another* sacrifice, but part of the same event. Attending the Eucharist is like being present at the original Last Supper with Jesus and the disciples.

Day 35

Mark 14.27-52: Gethsemane

Jesus takes Peter, James and John, the 'inner group' of disciples, to 'a place called Gethsemane', an olive grove on the western slope of the Mount of Olives. Since Judas knew where to find it, perhaps they had been there before.

There are several things to notice about verses 32-42:

— Jesus is absolutely terrified by the thought of the death that awaits him. He reacts as any other human being would. Yet he has the courage to go through with it.

— In his prayer, Jesus calls the Father 'Abba'. The Good News Bible translates this as 'My Father!' In fact, it means 'Dad' or 'Daddy' in Aramaic. Most people in Jesus' time thought you could not call God 'Abba' because it was not sufficiently respectful. Mark, however, thinks Jesus is so close to God that he can use this name. The early Christians took up the idea and they too called God 'Abba' (Romans 8.15: Galatians 4:6).

— The disciples are asleep. 'The spirit is willing, but the flesh is weak,' says Jesus: they want to stay awake, but are too exhausted.

— When trouble comes, even the disciples break. If Mark's first readers faced death because of their faith, they could draw strength from Jesus' example to go through with it in spite of their fear. But if they fail, there is comfort in knowing that the disciples were welcomed back by the risen Jesus, even though they had not held out to the end.

— Jesus tells the disciples to get up and go to meet 'the one who is betraying me'. Either he somehow realises that Judas is on his way, or perhaps he simply sees him in the distance.

Judas arrives with a gang of armed men, sent by the Sanhedrin. Perhaps they were the Temple guard, the Jewish police who kept order in the Temple, or a group of ordinary people. John seems to suggest that Roman soldiers were involved (John 18.3).

They have arranged a signal: the person to arrest is the one Judas kisses. A pupil would usually show his love and respect for his master by kissing him. Here, it seems to show exactly the opposite.

They arrest Jesus. There is a brief fight, and someone cuts off the ear of the High Priest's slave or servant. John says it was Peter (John 18.10). But Jesus is not an 'outlaw' or a man of violence. He is not a warrior Messiah. They could have arrested him at any time when he taught in the Temple, but they did not. The disciples run off, frightened that they will be arrested as well. In Mark, Jesus does not see them again before his death.

Mark includes something in this story which Matthew, Luke and John omit: he mentions the young man who followed Jesus (14.51-52). It is often said that this young man was actually Mark himself. This is an attractive idea, but there is no evidence for it. The young man may have been an eyewitness, who passed on his information. Or it may look back to Amos 2:16, which says that strong men would flee away naked when the Day of the Lord came. We do not know.

To consider:

'Not what I will, but what you will.'

Day 36

Mark 14.53-72: The trial before the Sanhedrin

The Sanhedrin, the Jewish council, was looking 'for some evidence against Jesus in order to put him to death'. The meeting was held in the High Priest's house, so where did Mark get his information from? This is not an easy question. Some scholars think that all of the details of the trial before the Sanhedrin were invented by the early Christians, who did not know exactly what happened. However, we know that some members of the Sanhedrin – Joseph of Arimathea, for example (Mark 15.43) and perhaps Nicodemus (John 3.1, 19.39) – were sympathetic towards Jesus. If they later became Christians they may have told others what had happened.

Mark says the witnesses gave false evidence. The first charge they try to fix on Jesus is speaking against the Temple: that he threatened to pull the Temple down and rebuild it. Any sensible court would throw out the idea. Was Jesus going to do it with his bare hands? In 13.2, Jesus had predicted the destruction of the Temple, but had not said *he* was going to do it. The witnesses seem to have confused the saying in 13.2 with a prediction of Jesus' resurrection, which would take place 'after three days' (see John 2.19-22). But the witnesses do not agree, and the charge has to be dropped.

Things are going on too long, so the High Priest stands up. In the time of Jesus, the High Priest was Caiaphas, although some people thought of his father-in-law Annas as the real High Priest. (Matthew says Caiaphas did the talking, although John suggests Annas was also involved: Matthew 26.57; John 18.13, 24.)

Is Jesus going to say nothing to the charges? On the surface, this seems fair enough. The 'charges' so far have been trumped-up nonsense; why should Jesus reply? However, Mark's readers would have remembered what the Book of Isaiah said about the Servant of the Lord:

> He was treated harshly but endured it humbly;
> he never said a word.
> Like a lamb about to be slaughtered,
> Like a sheep about to be sheared,
> He never said a word. (Isaiah 53.7)

This is just what happens to Jesus here. (It is also worth noting Psalms 27.12 and 35.11.)

The Sanhedrin is getting nowhere, so the High Priest tries a direct question. He asks Jesus point blank whether he is the Messiah, and receives the reply, 'I am, and you will see the Son of Man seated on the right of Power [a Jewish circumlocution for "God"] and coming with the clouds of heaven.'

For the first and last time in Mark, Jesus openly agrees that he is the Messiah. The Messianic secret is over. Jesus can now admit his identity because the passion has begun; the Messiah is not a political liberator, but the suffering Son of Man. The words 'I am' are the same words Jesus used in 6.50; God had called himself 'I am' when he spoke to Moses (Exodus 3.14).

The Sanhedrin will see the Son of Man sitting at the Father's right hand, and coming with the clouds of heaven. Jesus will (metaphorically) sit at God's right hand: he will share in what the Father does. This prediction of the parousia may reflect an early Christian belief that it would happen within the lifetime of the first generation of Christians. Or it may mean the Sanhedrin will 'see' – in the sense of 'understand' – that he will be at God's right hand, that he is the Son of Man who will eventually return on the clouds of heaven. They will come to realise who he really is.

The High Priest tears his robes, a ceremonial action required when he heard blasphemy. There is a historical problem at this point because although claiming to be the Messiah might be wrong, it was not blasphemy. Four solutions have been suggested to this:
1. The Sanhedrin were so desperate to get rid of Jesus that they did not care what the Law said.
2. Jesus was actually found guilty of being a false or lying prophet, which carried the death sentence (Deuteronomy 13.1-5).
3. The Sanhedrin took Jesus' words ('I am' and 'the Son of Man... seated on the right hand of Power') to mean that he was claiming authority that belonged to God. *This* was the blasphemy.
4. The early Christians did not know what really happened. All they knew was the Jesus was tried. They have filled in the gaps by inventing an account of the proceedings.

Jesus is found guilty, yet his one 'crime' was being the Messiah. The Temple guards beat him and spit at him. This may echo the prediction of the Servant of the Lord's suffering in Isaiah 50.6.

According to John 18.31, the Sanhedrin was not allowed to execute people. (This is backed up by evidence from Jewish documents.) So the Council gets ready to hand him over to Pontius Pilate, who will ratify and carry out the death sentence.

The story of Peter's denial is so well told that there is little to say.

It is, however, worth noting that this story can originally have come only from Peter himself; no other Christian was present as a possible source. As we have seen, a number of early Christian writers said Mark knew Peter; it may well then be that the story comes not just originally, but directly, from Peter.

To consider:

Peter is the original source for the story of the denial; he had the courage to admit to what he had done and not make excuses. Do we have such courage to admit to our own failings?

Day 37

Mark 15.1-20: The trial before Pilate

As the Church spread over the Roman Empire, Christian missionaries had to deal with the embarrassing fact that Jesus had been tried and condemned by a Roman governor. This could hardly be expected to go down very well with the Roman public and Mark may well have been written in the capital itself. So the Gospels tend to play down Pilate's part in the affair, making it clear that the Jewish authorities pushed him into a difficult situation.

The morning meeting of the Sanhedrin (15.1)

If the Sanhedrin has already condemned Jesus during the night (14.15-64), why does it meet again on Friday morning?

It seems most likely that it had to: a trial during the night was against the law. So the Sanhedrin had to meet again at daybreak in order to go through the case again and make the verdict legal.

The trial before Pilate (15.2-5)

'Inflexible, stubborn and cruel.' That was what the Jewish writer Philo called Pilate. He went on to say Pilate 'executed troublemakers without trial' and that he was guilty of 'violence, thefts, assault, abusive behaviour, constant executions and relentless, savage cruelty.'

Josephus, the Jewish historian, gives us more details. Pilate was a hard line and confrontational governor who despised the people he ruled. The Torah forbade images; Pilate's predecessors had usually respected local custom by veiling the Roman standards before they were brought into Jerusalem. Pilate thought this an affront to Roman prestige and had his troops bring the standards, unveiled, into the city by night. The Jews asked Pilate to remove them; Pilate refused. There was a stand-off for five days until Pilate lost patience, had his soldiers surround the Jews who were demonstrating, and threaten to kill them if they didn't back off. They told him to get on with it: they were not going to break the law of God and would rather die than do so. Pilate, wisely, gave in to their demands; he had nearly caused an uprising by being too harsh.

On another occasion, Pilate decided to build an aqueduct and looted the Temple treasury to do so. The Jews protested; Pilate had his troops infiltrate the crowd and beat up and kill a few of them to teach them a lesson.

In fact, this sort of thing got Pilate into trouble with his superiors and he was told to cool down. This may explain why he is less brutal in his dealings with Jesus than we might expect.

Mark does not tell us why Pilate asked Jesus if he was the 'king of the Jews'; presumably the Sanhedrin suggested it to him (see Luke 23.2). 'King of the Jews' is not actually a new idea; it's a perfectly reasonable translation of 'Messiah', though Pilate – like many Jews, in fact – would have understood it in political terms.

Jesus' reply is difficult. Literally, the Greek says, 'You are speaking.' This is sometimes translated as 'those are your words' or 'so you say', as though Jesus is neither agreeing nor disagreeing.

The release of Barabbas and Jesus' condemnation (15.6-15)

There has been a lot of debate about the story of Barabbas. Some scholars think that Mark told it this way in order to get Pilate off the hook. They would point out that we know a lot about Roman law and about the way the Romans ran Palestine, yet only the Gospel writers talks about a tradition of releasing prisoners at Passover time. (This assumes, of course, that the evangelists can't supply historically accurate information about such things. Lots of history, especially ancient history, is based on only one source.)

It has been suggested, then, that the Barabbas story grew out of the historical fact that someone called Barabbas was released, having been found not guilty, at the same time as Pilate was dealing with Jesus' case. The rest is an attempt to make the story of Jesus' death more acceptable to Roman readers.

There is, of course, the problem of eyewitnesses – crowds of them, in this case. If the facts were changed, somebody would surely have remembered what had really happened and contradicted Mark's story.

The story ends with a very brief note: Pilate had Jesus whipped. This was normal practice before somebody was crucified, but it was brutal. The weapon used was called a *flagellum*, which was made of several leather strips. Fastened to these were iron hooks. The victim was bent over, bound to a post, and then beaten. The *flagellum* caused horrific injuries.

The account as a whole echoes the Suffering Servant of Isaiah. It's worth considering two passages in particular:

He was oppressed, and he was afflicted,

yet he opened not his mouth;
like a lamb that is led to the slaughter,
and like a sheep that before its shearers is dumb,
so he opened not his mouth.
By oppression and judgement he was taken away...
stricken for the transgression of my people...

I gave my back to those who struck me,
and my cheeks to those who pulled out the beard;
I did not hide my face
from insult and spitting...

(Isaiah 53.7-8, 50.6)

To consider:

> *But he was wounded for our transgressions;*
> *crushed for our iniquities;*
> *upon him was the punishment that made us whole,*
> *and by his bruises we are healed.*
>   *(Isaiah 53.5)*

Day 38

Mark 15.21-39: The death of Jesus

Execution was common in ancient times. Many crimes carried the death penalty, although the method of execution differed from country to country. In the Roman Empire, if you were a citizen of Rome, you were beheaded. Criminals who were not Roman citizens were crucified.

Crucifixion was a dreadful punishment, a way of torturing someone to death. The criminal was stripped, and then flogged to soften him up. A large beam of wood – the horizontal bar of the cross – was strapped to his arms, and he was made to walk through the town to the place of execution. A notice, stating his crime, was hung round his neck or carried in front of him. The soldiers always took the longest route, so that as many people as possible would see the offender.

When they reached the place of execution, the victim was made to lie on the ground and his wrists were nailed or roped to the beam. The crossbar and the criminal were hoisted up and fixed in place on a large piece of wood planted in the ground. The notice was fixed to the cross, and the person's feet were either nailed or tied to a block which supported the weight of the body. It usually took several days to die.

Crucifixion victims were usually left until they died from suffocation. The way the victims hung forward on their crosses made it difficult for them to breathe, except by forcing themselves up with their wrists and feet in order to gulp in air. Eventually they weakened, the pain became too great, and they gave up the struggle. (To speed things up the Roman soldiers would sometimes break their legs. They could no longer push themselves up to breathe, and died very quickly. (Cf John 19.31-33.))

Jesus was beaten so badly that he could not carry his own crossbeam. We do not know who Simon of Cyrene was; he may have been a pilgrim, who had come to Jerusalem for the Passover. Mark may name him for another reason. Paul mentions a Christian named Rufus at Rome (Romans 16.13) and it may be that 'Alexander and Rufus' were known to Mark's Church. If so, Mark mentions Simon to show that his information came from an eyewitness.

Jesus is crucified at nine o'clock in the morning ('the third hour') at a place called Golgotha. 'Golgotha' is the Aramaic word for 'skull', which Mark translates for his Gentile readers. We are not sure exactly where it was. In Jerusalem today, you can visit the Church of the Holy Sepulchre, said to stand over Golgotha, but we cannot be sure this is the case as other sites have been suggested.

Two 'robbers' are crucified as well as Jesus. The word can mean 'revolutionaries'. Perhaps they were Zealots. Even at the end of his life, Jesus is found in the company of outcasts.

Someone offers him wine mixed with myrrh. This was a painkiller, but Jesus would not take it. The soldiers do not seem to care about the prisoner at all. They are playing dice to see who will get his clothes. Under Roman law, a crucified man's clothes belonged to his executioners. The notice stating Jesus' crime is hung on the cross: 'The King of the Jews'.

Jesus was crucified as a traitor. Perhaps Pilate's idea was to frighten any others who might claim to be the king of the Jews. Or perhaps he meant it as an insult to the Jewish authorities, which is suggested by John's Gospel (John 19.21-22). For Mark, that notice is important. Israel has rejected its king and the Romans do not recognise him. But the crucified 'criminal' really is the king of Israel.

The passers-by jeer at Jesus. The saying about the Temple comes up again (14.58). Nobody is interested in what Jesus really meant by it. They think he was boasting about his power. If he is so great, why does he not save himself? Even 'the chief priests and the teachers of the Law' mock him. If Jesus can come down from the cross, they say, then we'll believe in him — but they have totally missed the point. It is because Jesus stays on the cross that he is the Messiah. The Messiah has to suffer and die, not dazzle people with miracles.

At noon ('the sixth hour'), there is a 'darkness', which lasts for three hours. Mark may have an eclipse or a thunderstorm in mind but the darkness is symbolic: God is at work. In the Old Testament Book of Amos, God had said, 'I will make the sun go down at noon and the earth grow dark in daytime' (Amos 8.9).

Jesus has been on the cross for three hours, when he cries out, 'Eloi, Eloi, lama sabachthani?' Mark translates these Aramaic words for his readers: 'My God, my God, why hast thou forsaken me?' The words are a quotation from the first line of Psalm 22. There are two possible reasons why Jesus says this:

Psalm 22 is the prayer of someone in great trouble. Perhaps Jesus is thinking of the end of the psalm, where God saves the writer. He sums up the whole psalm by quoting the first line. God showed himself to be on the side of the psalm writer; he will show himself to be on the side of Jesus.

Or Jesus actually feels that God has abandoned him. Whatever else he was, Jesus was a human being, and he is dying. At this moment, Jesus took on himself the sins of the world. Sin puts up a barrier between people and God. On the cross, Jesus felt that barrier.

The people watching do not understand what the cry means. They mistake 'Eloi' for 'Elijah', and think that Jesus is calling for the prophet's help. Elijah would return at the time of the Messiah and some also believed he would come to help good people in trouble. Someone soaks a sponge in 'vinegar' (this may have been the mixture of egg, water and vinegar that Roman soldiers usually drank). The sponge is held up to Jesus' lips, and they wait to see if Elijah will come to his help. This may have been an act of kindness, but Mark seems to think it was a sick, half-joking experiment.

Jesus cries out, and dies.

At that moment, the Temple curtain is torn in two. This curtain hung in front of the Holy of Holies, the most sacred part of the Temple. The Holy of Holies was a symbol of God's presence among the Jewish people and only the High Priest could enter it, just once a year, on the Day of Atonement. But now the barrier has gone. What does this mean? Scholars have come up with three possible answers:

1. It is a sign that the Temple will be destroyed in the Jewish War. This was when the Romans finally destroyed Jerusalem in 70 AD.
2. It means that the barrier of sin which separates God from humankind has been removed by Jesus' death.
3. It means that the Temple, and Jerusalem, are no longer the places where people can find God. Jesus and the Kingdom have arrived. Now Gentiles as well as Jews are members of the people of God.

The centurion seems to realise who Jesus is. The Romans sometimes called their great heroes 'a son of God' or 'a son of the gods'. In Greek, his words can mean either of these; it may be the nearest he can get to saying who Jesus really is.

The first person to have faith in Jesus after his death is not a Jew, not a member of the authorities, and not even one of the disciples. It is a Gentile: an outsider, an outcast.

To consider:

Truly, this man was the Son of God.

Day 39

Mark 15.40-16.8: The resurrection

The women in verses 40-41 appear in the Gospel here for the first time, despite the fact that Mark says they were with Jesus in Galilee. Mark contrasts their faithfulness with the cowardice of the male disciples, who fled in Gethsemane.

Joseph of Arimathea asks Pilate for Jesus' body and buries it. Usually the Romans liked to leave the corpses of criminals hanging on their crosses, as a warning to others. However, this does not seem to have worked in Israel, where Jewish burial customs were very strict. Bodies had to be buried on the day of death, if at all possible. Josephus wrote that 'the Jews are so careful about funeral rites that even criminals who have been crucified are taken down and buried before sunset' (*The Jewish War*, IV:5:2).

So Joseph has to be quick, because it is also nearly the Sabbath, when even burying the dead was considered 'work' and was forbidden. There was not even time to anoint Jesus' corpse with the usual spices; it is simply wrapped up and placed in a tomb. A stone is rolled across the entrance.

The women come to the tomb once the Sabbath is over, and as soon as it is light. It was usual for a dead person's family and friends to visit the grave after the burial. Mark adds that they went there to anoint Jesus' body, which Joseph had not had time to do.

But Jesus is not there.

Instead, the stone has been rolled back and a 'young man ... wearing a white robe' is sitting inside. Mark almost certainly means an angel, which is what Matthew's version says (Matthew 28.2). Jewish writings of Mark's time often talk about angels as 'young men' and of heavenly beings as wearing white. The young man says to the women that Jesus has been raised, and that they must tell the disciples he is going ahead of them to Galilee. What Jesus said just before his arrest has come true: 'After I am raised to life, I will go to Galilee ahead of you' (14.28). In verse 7, the young man singles Peter out. This is probably because of his importance as the leader of the apostles but it is also because Peter has denied Jesus. He is not to worry about it: Jesus has forgiven him (cf John 21.15-19).

Despite the angel's attempt to calm them, the women are terrified. They run away and say nothing.

This is hardly surprising in the circumstances but the women's fear is important. It is the same sort of fear (but much more intense) as the disciples felt when Jesus calmed the storm (4.41). And it is the same kind of fear which made the Jews tremble, long before, at the signs of God's presence when he gave Moses the Ten Commandments (Exodus 20.18). The women's fear signals to Mark's readers that God, once again, is at work.

And that is where Mark's Gospel ends. No appearances of the risen Jesus. No moving, final meeting between Peter and Christ. Just a few terrified women, too frightened to speak, running away from Jesus' tomb.

It seems pretty abrupt.

A couple of writers in the second century thought so too. After all, Matthew, Luke and John all go on to tell stories about Jesus' appearances to his disciples in Galilee and Jerusalem. So these second century writers each had a go – not very successfully – at finishing Mark's Gospel off for him. You can read their attempts: they're printed in Bibles as Mark 16.9-20. But here, Mark ends. Perhaps he meant to carry on. Some scholars think he did. Maybe the original ending was lost. Most New Testament experts today, though, think Mark knew exactly what he was doing by stopping at this point. As he was the first Gospel writer, why shouldn't he end where he liked? And ending on a cliffhanger, at the most important point, is a good way to finish the book. After all, the message is out:

Jesus is risen.

To consider:

Jesus was not merely a good and great man who died a tragic and pointless death. The resurrection shows that he was indeed who he said he was, and that everything he taught was true.

Day 40

Mark 16.9-20: The added endings to Mark

As we saw, Mark ends with the women meeting the young man at Jesus' tomb:

> Trembling and bewildered, the women went out and fled from the tomb. They said nothing to anyone, because they were afraid.   (Mark 16.8)

We said that this is abrupt. Two Christian writers in the second century tried to finish off Mark's Gospel for him. The shorter addition reads:

> The women went to Peter and his friends and gave them a brief account of what they had been told. After this, Jesus himself sent out through his disciples from the east to the west the sacred and ever-living message of eternal salvation.

(Notice this contradicts what Mark has just said!)

There is also a longer, more detailed ending. Neither of these extra endings can have been written by Mark himself. The style of the Greek is too different and the best manuscripts leave them out completely.

The longer ending added to Mark (16.9-20)

As the longer ending goes into much more detail, we need to examine it in more depth.

We do not know who wrote it. A tenth Century document says it was written by someone called 'Ariston', but this 'evidence' is so late it's hardly reliable. However, we'll call the writer of 16.9-20 'Ariston' here: we have to call him something, and he certainly wasn't Mark! We'll keep 'Ariston' in inverted commas, though, as a reminder that we're not certain that was his name. Some manuscripts have extra material slotted in which we'll look at shortly.

'Ariston' does not do a very good job. He has either summarised material from the other Gospels (and introduced a few of his own, rather zany, ideas), or he originally wrote the account for some other reason, and then it's been added on to Mark's Gospel.

Whichever is the case, we can make the following points about 'Ariston's' work:

- The full versions of the appearances 'Ariston' mentions are in the other Gospels:
  Mary Magdalene: John 20.11-18
  The two travellers: Luke 24.13-35
  The eleven disciples: Luke 24.36-49, John 20.19-29.
- 'Ariston' says that the risen Jesus reminded his followers to preach the Gospel and to baptise new Christians.
- 'Ariston' believes that Jesus gave the Christians powers to drive out demons, heal people, speak in strange tongues, pick up snakes with their bare hands and drink deadly poison. It was commonly believed in the early Church that the first three happened in their communities. The last two look as though they've come from the lunatic fringes of early Christianity. Some modern Christians have tried to explain away the ideas' strangeness: they suggest they're imagery for coping heroically with life's troubles. This is certainly not the obvious meaning. Except for a very few extreme groups, modern Christians do not drink poison or handle venomous snakes as part of their worship.
- Many fundamentalist and conservative Christians have a fairly liberal approach to 'Ariston's' work. They would tend to accept the parts which are backed up by the other Gospels, but ignore the more eccentric aspects. After all, as it was added on later to Mark, it is not really part of the Bible. So it has no real authority.

'Ariston' says Jesus 'was taken up into heaven' after he had appeared to the disciples. Luke says that the risen Jesus appeared to the disciples for forty days (a round number, meaning 'a bit more than a month' – see Acts 1.3). At the end of this, Jesus stopped appearing to his disciples. To show that the appearances had ended, Luke says Jesus ascended into heaven (Luke 20.50-53, Acts 1.6-11). Not all Christians take it literally. It can be understood as imagery: Jesus 'returns' to be with God, and his disciples will no longer see him directly.

One Greek manuscript of Mark includes some extra material after 16.14. This material is called the *Freer Logion*, after the owner of the manuscript. It is written in pretty bad Greek, but as far as we can tell, this is what it says:

> They said to Christ, 'Nobody keeps the laws today and nobody believes anything. Satan is in charge. People do not understand God's true power, because Satan's evil spirits are stopping them. So, you must make people see what is holy and right immediately.'

Christ answered, 'The time of Satan's rule is over. But even the sinners I died for will suffer other terrible things. These will make them turn to the truth and stop sinning. Then they will go to heaven, and share in the spiritual holiness that will last for ever.'

Not very inspiring, and not very convincing either. These words are very different from anything Mark ever wrote or, as far as we can tell, Jesus ever said. Most experts say they were written in the second or third centuries. It's clear that, for whoever wrote them, the Church was going through a bad patch. People wanted to know why everybody didn't become Christians and why the parousia had not yet happened. The idea that sinners need to suffer more on earth, as though Jesus' death was not enough to effect the atonement, is less than Christian. Clearly some early Christians believed such nonsense, but this idea has no place in Christianity today.

To consider:

'If Christ has not been raised, then our proclamation has been in vain and your faith has been in vain... If Christ has not been raised, your faith is futile and you are still in your sins... If for this life only we have hoped in Christ, we are of all people most to be pitied.

But in fact Christ has been raised from the dead, the first fruits of those who have died. For since death came through a human being, the resurrection of the dead has also come through a human being.'

(Paul in 1 Corinthians 15.14, 17, 19-21)

Did the resurrection really happen?

We're living, in the West at least, in an age where religious belief is increasingly seen as old fashioned, out of date and, worse, stupid and politically incorrect. The rise of what has been called 'aggressive atheism' has led to some very successful and badly argued books, shrieking with rage against Christianity and all it stands for. There are those who assume it is impossible to have a brain and to be religious; all philosophy which argues in favour of God's existence, and all theology, are ignored and swept away as dangerous rubbish. The history of Western thought is ignored – and, if it won't go away, it is shouted at.

To some extent, there is nothing new in this. Atheism is not a new doctrine. What is new is the shrillness with which popular writers rail against religion. The days seem to be gone when atheists and theists could debate their views courteously and with mutual respect.

This section is offered as a counter-argument to some of the new atheists' ideas. There are many arguments in favour of Christianity and the existence of God. One of the key ones is the evidence for saying that the resurrection of Jesus is a genuine historical event. The points discussed below are not new; they represent a summary of what leading Christian writers and thinkers have said.

The whole of Christianity stands or falls on the idea that Jesus really rose from the dead. If that never happened, then Christianity is untrue and Jesus may be a decent man who taught some attractive things about being morality, but that's it. (And Jesus would have been wrong in almost everything he said about every other topic, too.)

Did it happen? Did Jesus rise from the dead?

We have to be careful what we mean. Some of the *accounts* of what the risen Jesus did or said may contain some features which are not historical (Mark 16.9-20 has some unhistorical details). We're not asking whether every detail the Gospels describe is correct. The question is just: did Jesus rise from the dead, or not?

When Christianity talks about Jesus 'rising from the dead', it does not mean resuscitating a corpse. Jesus did not have his heart re-started. The resurrection is something to do with God, and, as is so often when people talk about God, they have to use picture language.

So the risen Jesus is said to have been raised to a new type of life. He would never die again; he was immortal. Paul says he had a 'spiritual body'. He was clearly the same person, because his disciples recognised him. (John's Gospel says the risen Jesus proved this point to Thomas by showing him the marks in his hands and side.) Yet his body was also different in certain ways: he could appear in a room when the doors were locked (John 20.19), and his followers didn't always recognise him at first (Luke 24.30-32. 'Ariston' seems to have the same idea in Mark 16.12). We do not know exactly what the Gospel writers think the risen Jesus looked like. But then, they don't tell us what Jesus looked like before his resurrection, either.

But did it happen?

No serious scholar now doubts that the earliest Christians genuinely *believed* it did. Professor E. P. Sanders, a leading liberal New Testament scholar, is certain that the disciples genuinely *believed* they had experiences of the risen Jesus. (To be fair to Professor Sanders, he goes on to say that he does not know what the disciples *actually* experienced.)

'Did Jesus really rise from the dead?' is partly a question about whether something happened in history. If it's true, it's something that really happened. If it's true, there should be good grounds historically for saying that it took place.

Normally, if a historical source said a dead man walked, we'd just dismiss it as ridiculous. In the case of Jesus, though, it's so important to Christianity that it's worth investigating carefully.

Maybe miracles can happen; maybe they can't. Different people have different ideas. If we start from the position that there is no God, and the resurrection of Jesus is utterly impossible, then there's no point in debating it. But is the evidence strong enough, if we keep an open mind, to show that Jesus rose from the dead?

If Jesus did *not* rise from the dead, then what *did* happen?

Various theories have been put forward and we examine them here.

Theory 1: Jesus survived his crucifixion and faked his own resurrection.

This sounds quite reasonable, until you start to think about it. It assumes that the Roman execution squad were unrealistically stupid, and couldn't tell the difference between a dead man and someone who was unconscious. (Wouldn't they have checked his pulse?) John's Gospel says the Romans made quite sure that Jesus was dead:

they thrust a lance into his body, presumably aiming for the heart (John 19.31-35). Although it's *just about* possible that someone *just might* survive that, the question has to be asked: *is it likely?*

It also makes Jesus a fraud and a liar. He *might* have been, but there is no evidence. It goes against what we know of the sort of man he was. Even very liberal New Testament scholars would hesitate at saying Jesus was a fraud. Again, the question is: is it likely?

Even if Jesus *could* have survived, what sort of shape would he have been in? We know what appalling mutilation crucifixion caused to the human body. Would someone suffering from awful injuries, who was barely alive, really have convinced his disciples he had risen from the dead? (And how would he have escaped from the tomb? It was sealed by a huge stone.)

Theory 2: Someone stole the body.

The Jews or the Romans could have stolen the body of Jesus. Or the disciples did.

If the Jews or the Romans did it, perhaps they wanted to stop the disciples themselves from stealing it. They wanted to prevent the disciples from faking Jesus' resurrection.

Or the disciples did it to do just that.

But if the Jews or the Romans took the body, where did it go? The Jewish authorities hated the new religion of Christianity, and attacked it from the beginning. (The Acts of the Apostles gives the details.) The Romans did not like Christianity either.

All they had to do to destroy the religion would be to produce the body. No missing body, no resurrection of Jesus. No resurrection of Jesus, no Christianity. End of story.

But they didn't produce the body. This almost certainly means that they hadn't got it.

The theory of the stolen body doesn't make sense for what we know about life in those days; it does not take account of the historical context. For Jews, dead bodies were revolting. Touching one made you religiously unclean, according to the Torah. The disciples were Jews. Their religious sense would have been too strong to allow them to fool around with a dead body. Moreover, the Jewish historian Josephus tells us that Jerusalem – quite a small town by today's standards – was absolutely packed with pilgrims during Passover. This was when Jesus was buried. Moving a dead body around unnoticed would have been impossible.

The disciples would have believed in a general resurrection – that, at some fixed point in the future, *all* the dead would rise and be judged by God. Yet *no-one* believed that only *one* man would rise. So, they would not have believed that Jesus would rise from the dead, and would not have a motive to fake it. Mark says that they did not have the faintest idea what Jesus was talking about when he predicted his resurrection (Mark 9.9-10).

In fact, some scholars have suggested this point gives one good reason for saying that the resurrection *did* happen. No-one expected it, so no-one would fake it. The Messiah was expected to kill other people, not die and rise again. A good reason for making people change their view – and saying *one* man *had* risen – was that it happened.

The natural reaction to finding an empty tomb would be to assume the body had been stolen. (John says this is what Mary Magdalene thought – see John 20.11-18.) Careful study of the New Testament shows that faith in Jesus' resurrection was not originally based on an empty tomb. Paul, writing in AD 54 to the Church at Corinth, lists the people to whom he says the risen Jesus appeared (1 Corinthians 15.3-8). He says that most of them were still alive when he was writing (so presumably he's saying to his readers: go and ask them). Paul bases his belief in the resurrection on the *appearances* of the risen Jesus. *He never mentions an empty tomb.* He did not think it was important.

New Testament scholars say this shows belief in Jesus' resurrection was *not* based on the empty tomb. It was based on the idea that Jesus appeared.

The concept of the empty tomb was only appealed to later, to back up the idea of the resurrection. This is the picture we find in the Gospels. An empty tomb alone would not make people believe the resurrection.

(Does Mark say the women said 'nothing to anyone' (16.8) to show that the tomb's being empty wasn't that important – that the women never reported it?)

Matthew says the Jewish leaders asked Pilate to set up a guard on Jesus' tomb to prevent the disciples from stealing the body (Matthew 27.62-66). If this detail is correct, how would the disciples have got past a squad of armed men?

Theory 3: Someone else was crucified instead of Jesus. Jesus then faked his own resurrection.

Once again, this makes Jesus a fraud and a liar. We have seen the problems with this idea.

And, once again, it makes the Romans total idiots. Jesus was well known. Wouldn't someone have noticed? John's Gospel says Jesus' mother and the Beloved Disciple (usually thought to be John) stood at the foot of the cross and were able to speak to Jesus (John 19.25-27). Surely they would have recognised him?

And when would the switch have taken place? Wouldn't the Sanhedrin have protested at the Romans' incompetence when they saw it was not their enemy being executed, but someone else?

Theory 4: The risen Jesus was actually someone else pretending to be Jesus.

But wouldn't they have noticed? People were no more gullible then than they are now.

Theory 5: The disciples believed they had seen the risen Jesus, but they were mistaken.

Perhaps, in their grief at Jesus' death, they made it all up. Or they hallucinated (perhaps they were on drugs).

Yet the risen Jesus did not behave like a hallucination. Hallucinations happen to individuals, not groups. They're usually incoherent, not coherent. Hallucinations can't be touched, and certainly can't cook you breakfast (Luke 24.36-39, John 21.1-14).

The disciples' being on drugs initially sounds more plausible. Magic mushrooms did grow in Israel.

There is only one drawback: there is no evidence that they used drugs.

And in any case, the accounts of the appearances of the risen Jesus are nothing like accounts drug users have written of their 'trips'.

The idea that the disciples made it all up is unrealistic. Professor E. P. Sanders draws attention to the Romans' usual practice. If you executed a troublemaker, you rounded up all his followers and executed them as well. That the Romans initially left the disciples alone shows that they did not regard Jesus as a very great threat. The disciples would have been terrified, believing that they were next. And they thought Jesus' execution was the end. He wasn't the Messiah after all, he was wrong, he'd died crying out to his God, who had abandoned him.

Men in that state of mind do not make up stories about their dead leader being alive again.

We also know that many of the disciples (including Peter) were executed for being Christians. Would they really be willing to die for something they had made up?

Jesus was killed on Friday. By Sunday evening, something had happened. Something which convinced broken men that Jesus had won, not lost. Something which they were willing to die for. Whatever had happened to effect this monumental change, it had to have been something absolutely extraordinary.

Theory 6: Jesus was from outer space. Or he was a time traveller.

Jesus' superior technology made the disciples think he had risen from the dead.

It's pretty extraordinary that people suggest ideas like these, but they do. There is only one tiny problem with them: there is no evidence. (However, people who are willing to believe such ideas usually do not bother with evidence.)

What makes most sense? What is most likely?

If we assume that nothing outside our own experience can possibly happen, we get nowhere. If it happened, the resurrection of Jesus *would be* outside our normal experience because, of the billions of people who have ever lived, *only one* rose from the dead. If it happened, it must be outside our normal experience. It only ever happened once.

History never allows us to be 100% certain. Henry VIII could have had a seventh wife whom he kept quiet about. We have to ask: what is the most likely explanation?

The Greek philosopher Aristotle said:

A plausible impossibility
is preferable to
an unconvincing possibility.

In other words:
- an explanation which makes sense, but which we'd normally consider impossible,

can be more convincing than:

- an explanation which is possible, but which is unconvincing.

150

In the present writers' view, the historical evidence points in one direction and it does so very clearly. This evidence has convinced some of the finest minds that Christianity is true and that it is based on the historical fact. To say that Jesus rose from the dead is not to utter a nonsensical belief in the teeth of the evidence. It is something that a cool consideration of the debate clearly points to. Jesus is risen.

Also available from St Mark's Press:

MARK'S GOSPEL on CD

NIV text

'This is the real thing... Peter Wickham's brilliant reading'
Sue Arnold in *The Guardian*

Peter Wickham's superb reading captures the power and drama of
Mark's story. Listening to a Gospel is a different experience from
reading it; indeed, it's highly likely that it was the way the first
Christians experienced Mark: as something that they heard, rather
than as something that they read. The Bible's often read in small
extracts, which are then subjected to intense analysis. It's easy to
forget that each book has its own story, style and drama – all
conveyed very effectively by this beautifully read recording.

Peter Wickham's acting career encompasses an enormous amount of
work for theatre, film and radio. As a member of the BBC Radio
Drama company, Peter has been in over a hundred radio plays, and
he has made over 250 audio books. He brings this great experience
to this recording of Mark's Gospel. It is a pleasure to listen to.

For every copy sold, a £1 donation is made to Christian Aid.

ISBN 978-1-907062-01-8
£12.99

William Barclay books from St Mark's Press

THE GOSPELS AND ACTS

Volume One: Matthew, Mark and Luke
Volume Two: John and Acts

Masterly: two of the best books on the New Testament ever written.

Professor Barclay's study of the Gospels and Acts takes the reader
effortlessly, gently and wisely through the theories, speculation,
guesswork – and findings – of New Testament studies. This two